Mail and Grow Rich

How To Get Rich
in
"Mail Order" in the *Information Age*

by

Ted Ciuba

MAIL AND GROW RICH

How To Get Rich
in
"Mail Order" in the *Information Age*

by Ted Ciuba
© 2000 by Ted Ciuba, *all rights reserved*

ISBN: 0-9672414-0-5

Published by:

Parthenon Marketing, Inc.
2400 Crestmoor Rd #36
Nashville, Tennessee 37215
U.S.A.

http://www.mailandgrowrich.com
talk@mailandgrowrich.com

Orders & Enrollments:
1-877- *4 RICHES*
***
+615-662-3169
fax: +615-662-3108

Ted Ciuba is available for speeches, lectures, workshops, copywriting, and marketing consulting. Please contact publisher.

Every friend is a friend for life!

Everyday vanilla uncomplicated
21ˢᵗ Century technology. – Ted Ciuba

Sitting In Your Spare Bedroom,
Your Business Spans The Planet! – Ted Ciuba

All who are ready may learn, not only <u>what</u> to do,
but also <u>how</u> to do it... and receive, as well,
the needed <u>stimulus</u> to make a start!
– Napoleon Hill, *Think and Grow Rich*

– In Memoriam –
Dedicated to you, Beloved Mother,
Shirley Marian Ciuba

Y a tí, Ana de mi vida

Table of Contents

MAIL AND GROW RICH
by Ted Ciuba

The MAIL AND GROW RICH System

Ted Ciuba, Marketer,
Marketing Consultant

Gives You A Realistic, Low Cost, Low Risk, Complete Step-By-Step *Proven* Mail Order System That **Anyone** **Can** **Use** To Instantly Accomplish *Financial Independence* Starting *Today!*

Dear Friend:

No matter how broke you are right now, I want you to know that I've been there. I was living in a single-axle camper trailer that I paid $500 for. I had it parked on the county line in a trailer park for $35 a month. The kind where the big dogs run around all night... At the end of a long country dirt road in rural Tennessee. Them rednecks there pay taxes on their wages, pack an array of guns, and still fly rebel flags from their trailers. And they *mean* it. Detectives and bill collectors are definitely not welcome.

They didn't repossess my car, because I outran them. I disappeared overnight for the promised land, California. I know what it means to encounter adverse circumstances. (Of course I settled accounts later, and moved back to Nashville... When you *have* money, it's easy...)

Things Have Changed - You Can Have A Million Dollar Income

No matter what your present circumstances, if you aspire to a million dollar income, I'm here to assure you, it's entirely within your ability to make it happen! *Easily. Enjoyably.*

There Is No Better Way To Get Rich Today
Than In Taking Advantage of the Gifts
the Information Age Has Given Us

To get started, you simply need a high profit product and proven order-sucking copy. Together we'll make sure you get that. You can do everything from home, using your phone, the fax, your computer, and the neighborhood copy machine.

Any ordinary first-world mortal can go into the "mail order" business today. It's simply the best, easiest, cheapest, most trouble-free, outrageously liberating, most profitable business on Planet Earth!

As an English language speaker, pop a site up on the internet and you're operating a global business! People from Australia, Europe, South America, Asia, and Russia are sending you their money, *eager to own American products*! (All conveniently billed to the 16 digits of their credit card number! *Ahh!*) This is how easy it is!

The Block-Buster Marketing Event of the 21st Century!

And when you sell these same customers products from your "backend," you increase your overall profits by 300%-400%-3,000% or more! And, *crème-de-la-crème*, when you decide it's time to really amp up your income, combine good marketing with products of your own!

Putting the powerful principles I'm revealing to you into effect, I enjoyed *instant* success! *Everything* turned around with my first ad. A *free* classified on America Online. Within weeks I had money, time, ability to relax and *enjoy* life, relationships, love, family life, vacations, houses, cars, friends, prestige... And it's only continued to get better!

Once I found the magic formula you're about to learn, what I had been searching for years overwhelmed me so fast that I didn't even know it hit me! I didn't know when I earned my first $100,000 or when I hit my first $1,000,000 until after I hired an attorney and a C.P.A. to help me make sense of the prosperity!

Imagine! Both $100,000 and $1,000,000 had been landmark goals of mine every day of my life for years, and I *shot* right past them without struggle!

That's what the super power of "Mail Order" in the *Information Age* Can Do For *You!*

Mail and Grow Rich!

[signature]

Ted Ciuba, Marketer, Marketing Consultant
1 January 2000
Santafé de Bogotá, Colombia

P.S. Imagine the freedom that is yours! ...the freedom of knowing your future years are sustained... ...the freedom of multi-million dollar bank accounts... ...private schools and university educations... ...travel to Bermuda, Switzerland, and the Galapagos, sharing true love with your family, and not worrying about the cost! Imagine the freedom!!!

You've just found it!

## Chapter 1

Secrets To Earning
$3,288
In Less Than 1 Hour

You know the *problem* well. **MONEY!**

We're *not* talking about your money problems anymore...

What we're talking about is *SOLUTIONS*...

We're going to cover a lot of separate topics in this densely valuable book, but it all concerns only *you* and the solution...

Money!

That's all. Money. And *you*. Lots of money. *Enjoyably. Easily.* I'm going to teach you to do exactly what I'm doing. Raking in the cashola with nary a penney's worth of effort. You're going to unleash incredible new levels of *leverage* in your business life – and indeed, in your *personal life*, too!

If I've done my job right, you'll never be the same after engaging this book. We're talking about *YOU* getting <u>rich</u> *in mail order*. <u>Today</u>! *Really Rich*.

But first, what's the hottest thing going today? It's the internet, isn't it? And there's a reason why Bill Gates, head of Microsoft, is the richest man in the world today, isn't there? It's the *computer*. Technology is making billionaires!

You can get your share!

Technology and Communications Advances Have Made It Possible For The Little Guy One Man Home-Office To Compete In The World Marketplace!

But you don't need to be a Bill Gates or a computer wizard to quickly, easily, and safely become a millionaire today. All you need are basic technology tools that will transform you from the old horse-and-buggy days of "mail order" (when it truly got its name), to what we now call *direct response marketing.*

Basic technology – nothing "techie," no programming... Stuff so simple your 3rd grade child could do it.

That's what you're going to get out of this little book. The absolute cutting edge disarmingly simple but powerful insider secrets that can make you a millionaire inside of a few years. With hardly any work or stress.

"It's Better To Be Rich Than Poor"

It's not really that hard to make a million dollars today... One out of every 100 people living in the United States are millionaires. Statistics say every 5 minutes another one joins them. Why not you?

Forget any old programming you may have learned from rich churches and broke teachers that taught you to fear money. Money is easily accessible. And money is *great!*

I like what Ben Suarez, the Hispanic mail order make-good says about it. Rumor has it – *he's not talking* – that he's pulling in some years $70,000,000. He has quite an operation churning in Canton, Ohio.

Oh, by the way, the Hispanics are another group that is "supposed" to be disenfranchised. Maybe they are as far as working a job or a government giveaway. No comment. But Ben Suarez sure proves that color and race have <u>nothing</u> to do with your success.

You just have to know how it's done.

Read his book, *7 Steps To Freedom II*, and you'll see that he too, like most mail order success stories, including possibly yourself, started with a lousy job, a big desire, and a little effort. In his determined search he encountered *mail order*, and was able to optimize his way into the giant success he enjoys today.

He writes:

> I can tell you from experience: It is *BETTER TO BE RICH THAN POOR*. I've been both places, and I can't emphasize this enough: It is much better to be your own boss and control your own destiny than to answer to people who direct your life for their own self-serving purposes. It is better to have a life doing what you want to do. *It is much better to be rich than poor.*
>
> If an individual was miserable when poor, he or she will be miserable when rich also. I had fun during both periods. My institutional career made me miserable at times, but still, I had fun when I was poor, and I had fun at the early stages of starting my enterprise. As a family, *we were always happy.* Yet, *we are happier rich.*

> Make no mistake about it, money is in no way everything. There are a lot of other things you need to be "totally happy." Religion, family, friends, and personal achievement are important, too...
> **But *when you have money, they're even better.***

Everything goes better with MONEY!

You'll find as you read this book that it's actually, <u>very easy</u> to make $100,000 per year in mail order. *If you know how it's done!* And if you want more, it's there, too. Approached mindfully, it's shamefully easy to earn a million dollars a year. If your targets are somewhat lower, like an extra $1,000-$2,000 per month, that's fine, too. If you find these sums hard to believe right now... stick with me.

> *What is the best way in the world... the best real no b.s. way... to make a lot of money... if you are starting with nothing?*
> ***Direct Mail!***
> – Gary Halbert

I assure you, with the knowledge you'll get from *Mail and Grow Rich*, if you only put 1/100th of it into action, you will get rich.

There is no easier way to make a *LOT* of money quickly and *safely* than in mail order. I've tried everything... But I'm not the only one saying this. Everyone who's done it sings the same tune!

E. Joseph Cossman, multi-millionaire businessman and mail order baron says:

I know of no business in the world that requires such a small investment to start, yet holds promise of such tremendous financial gains as mail order.

The eccentric Gary Halbert, who routinely makes fortunes for himself and his clients is equally direct when he says:

What is the best way in the world... the best real no b.s. way... to make a lot of money... if you are starting with nothing? *Direct Mail!*

And you can do it with products that serve any market!

"$3,288.90 In Less Than 1 Hour!"

Indeed, the world is changing, and *today* you have an opportunity to share in that world!.

Excuse me. It's 9:06 a.m. and I've just been interrupted by the beautiful sound of the fax. I'm sitting at my desk in Nashville, Tennessee writing these very words you see. There're only 3 easy steps on level ground between my desk and my fax. A distributor is faxing in a $1,047 order.

It's so nice of him to do that for me. He lives in Midland, Texas, but his website, of course, spans the globe. A man from Ft. Lauderdale, Florida called him up. Then the distributor faxes me the credit card info in and, *Voila!* that money's in *MY* bank account!

Do you see how today's simple technology tools interact? The client saw the product on the *internet*, used the *phone* to order it, and our distributor uses the *fax* to transmit the order. I use my *computer*'s modem to run the credit card. Later today I'll copy the manuals at the *Insty-Print*. I don't have any of my own money tied up, I'll use the *customer*'s money that's already in my bank account to pay for the printing. (Hang around, I'll talk more about publishing-on-demand.) Finally, I'll tell *UPS* to deliver it. These are the only tools you need!

> *The fact is that more money has been made in direct marketing than any other business opportunity in history.*
> – Kevin Trudeau

Nothing to it!

I don't know of an easier and more profitable business in the world! Remember that I didn't do any "work" to earn this money:

BINGO! You're living **wealth principle #1 – *Multiplication!***

Get *away from selling your <u>time</u>...* to selling something *independent* of your time and effort... ...get **into *making a profit!***

We set the website up for the distributor, by the way. Now he's churning in orders like this nearly every day. We can help you the same way. I'll be sure and give you more details later.

Anyway... to continue!

Throughout this book I'm going to share a number of true stories. Everytime I do, *imagine that you are the character in each story.* Why? There's a variety of reasons.

1st: Psychologists, and Napoleon Hill, tell us that what we "see" for ourselves tends to come true.

2nd: *You <u>can</u> be the person in each of these stories!*

In truth, none of these stories are of exceptional people or exceptional accomplishment. Normal people who, because they had a vision (refer to sentence above), took a little step... The step of action. What happened was a *result*.

See it first, that is the law.

And it's become *so easy!* Anyone who will dare to use today's simple technology can easily match each of these accomplishments.

The truth is that there are individuals and companies raking in millions of dollars every week in this business. The big mail order houses, for instance, like Columbia Music Club. Or Lilian Vernon ...But we're talking about ordinary folks like you and me.

But first, excuse me again. I've just been delightfully interrupted by the sound of the fax again! I just can't keep my composure when that beautiful fax emits that abbreviated *ring*. Next comes the *whirr-r-r* of a nice fat order. *Hmm*. This order has been passed on to me by one of our distributors in Connecticut. A lady on the opposite coast, in Inglewood, California wants to start with our Paper Profit$ I & II. A $247.90 order. ☺

You Can Be Dumb Or Dumber And Still Succeed In This Business!

Once I was dumb. Technology dumb. Even the word "technology" sounded high-tech to me. I was poor, too. Then I stumbled my way in. Easily... over the course of a few months I became rich and independent.

It started when I saw lots of "normal people" with the ability to use the fax. So I asked one of them to help me. Five minutes later I knew how to send and receive faxes.

I needed to know about marketing. So I went to a mail order seminar and sent for some direct response marketing courses. Following the simple instructions I'd received, I wrote a classified ad and a 15 page sales letter. But this time they had the sure-fire power elements I needed to win. And win I did. A few weeks later I quit my lousy job. That was several years ago. I got rich in the first few months.

Please excuse me again. ...It's 10:02 a.m. I've just been interrupted by my email software. It talks to me every time an order comes in. Another distributor sending in another $997 order. This guy lives in South Carolina and has a customer from a neighboring state, North Carolina. His client completed the secure on-line registration on his site. Then he forwarded the order to me. Total internet technology. Everyday vanilla uncomplicated 21st Century technology.

It's 10:05 a.m. As I was saying........

Oh, I'm sorry. **Please excuse me one final time.** After I take this telephone call I promise I'm going to get my laptop and go down to the first floor and write on the dining room table. Away from the profitable diversions of the phone and the fax and the computer.

But first... This is an affiliate on the line who we helped go independent. He enrolled in the full *Paper Profit$* program at $737 a few months ago. Doing exactly what the manuals explained to him, Scott Pentecost earned a smacking **$42,629.15 on his first deal**. Today he wants me to take his credit card number to the tune of $997.00. Hey, he's seen what our programs can do for a person. *Especially a guy like himself. (Who is a guy exactly like yourself.)*

You've seen it all... Some people prefer to use the phone. Others like to use the fax. Others like the convenience of doing everything on the internet – those orders come in by email. Others, like you and me, orchestrate your profit-taking using all the mediums of communication. They all make you money.

....

Whew! That's better. Now that I'm downstairs I'll be able to write without thinking about all the money that I'm earning.

I had a friend show me in 30 minutes how to surf the worldwide web. Later I took a class at the community college to build a simple web site. Then I scanned a couple of books on internet marketing at Barnes and Noble.

Believe me. It's not important to have a whiz-bang web site that will purr-and-cat and whiz-and-bang... In fact, that could work against you. The important thing is marketing. My site is simple.

That's why I'm sharing my story with you. Not because I'm a particularly good internet guru. But I still make a bit of money off the web. In total, well over 60% of our business is in some way web-related. Hey, it's the 21st Century, the New Millennium! You can do the same thing.

It also illustrates the simple truth which is, *Get going!* The internet is so happening that today any moderately executed internet business can give you an independent living. If you want more, the internet will serve it up on a silver platter!

Review: Let's remind ourselves of a few things we just saw happening in this real life event. (By the way, I do have all the supporting documents on file, just in case the Big Boys question my claims.)

I just made $3,288.90 in less than 1 hour. But I can't say it was for "work." I didn't do a single bit of work to have this money come in! In fact, each order was a delightful interruption of the work I was trying to get done. Distributors and the information highway did all the work for me on 3 of the orders. On the 4th I simply chatted on the phone a little bit, concerning internet marketing. No high-pressure sales.

Everyone of these orders was generated from the internet. My costs, after putting up my $100 per year web site, are totally zero. When you don't have to spend any big bucks to market, it *sure makes it easy!*

Everyone benefits in this marketing maneuver. The client who buys the product receives the highest value instruction available today! This is where millionaires are born. The distributors each make a healthy profit. Marketing on the internet, expenses are *zero*, so when a distributor gets $300, that's a good hour's work.

Myself, the licensor, as the writer of the copy and some of the products, I make a pleasing profit on every transaction, without doing any work. This is one of the things I like best about writing, hiring, or commissioning an ad or product. **You do the work (or pay the bill) once, but it pays off for *years!*** Talk about *leverage*!

> *I know of no business in the world that requires such a small investment to start, yet holds promise of such tremendous financial gains as mail order.*
> – E. Joseph Cossman

Finally, the joint venture partners who supply the outside products, have just made another sale (and got another *paying* client!) with no effort on their own part. Win, win, win, win.

There's money for everyone who wants it in the information age today.

What makes it all work? A combination of savvy marketing and today's simple technology tools.

When you study the *Mail and Grow Rich* System you will have all the marketing savvy you need to write the same kind of killer classifieds and sales letters that I do. And technology? Not much... The phone, the fax, the computer, and the internet are the only technology tools in this true slice of life this very moment as I write these words. And they're *easy* to master.

The biggest part, however, is knowing *how* to use the technology tools. *Lots* of people know more than me about the internet and the computer. Lots of people can do things I can't. But I make a lot more money than any university computer professor I've ever heard of. Indeed, it's the marketing that makes money. All hours of the day and night people sending you orders like crazy!

Talk about the *Information Age! That*'s the kind of *information* I like! Those little digital impulses that transfer $97, $300, or $1,000 directly into your bank account, without your intervention or knowledge that it's even happened. Yahoo! for the *Information Superhighway*! Today *anyone* can earn BIG Bucks!

Continuing, 2 of the 4 orders are for *joint venture* products. A "joint venture" simply means selling the product of another... Like selling Ron LeGrand's Real Estate *Cash-Flow System* or Brian Keith Voiles *Advertising Magic*. Joint ventures can make you wealthy in short order!

You know I like the money flowing in this way while I do nothing but kick back and design even *another* product that will make me even more money! And, if you'll simply implement the things I'm sharing with you, *you can have identically the same experience!*

Well, that just about wraps up this writing session. I'm going back upstairs to the 4th floor and "work" a little.

I'm a lot richer now than I was when I sat down an hour ago. My $3,288.90 for an hour's worth of hanging out is *greater than a month's take-home pay* for *millions* of "successful" Americans!

I can't wait to get the real __mail__! Who knows how much I'll have waiting for me there?

Are you ready for your share?

You²

I really value my time with my family, so I only allow myself a few hours "work" each day – if you can call doing what you passionately love to do "working" – yet that business earns me more than $3,000 per hour.

When you learn the success secrets of mailorder, you find that the amount of money you make is *NOT* connected to the number of hours you put in.

If you'll read to the end of this book, you'll find out exactly how you can get identically the same system up and running – chugging out thousands of dollars for you while YOU *enjoy* life!

Don't get me wrong... $3,288.90 is not solely the impressive thing... Although I'm sure you won't mind marking your success in $3,000 hours... or $3,000 days. Or $4,000 days. $10,000 days. But what you'll like the most is that, unlike a job, all this money floods in with little active effort on your part!

Success Can Be Yours

The good news is that the difference between success and failure in life is no more than 4". The space between your ears. No, no thicker than 4 pages, the number of pages in a successful direct mailout. In fact, Gary Halbert blasted from poverty to millionairedom on the fuel of a *1 page* letter. (Stay tuned, because when I talk later about "The 2 Greatest Sales Letters In The World," this is one of them.)

Actually, the difference between success and failure is even less than the thickness of a letter...

I would like to say the difference is in the information you'll learn in this book... After all, this book contains the proven secrets that are currently earning thousands of adventurous and fulfilled homebased entrepreneurs *millions of dollars!* It's true you can't succeed without this secret knowledge.

But that's not telling the whole story, either. The difference is really in what drove you to purchase this book, and in what drives you to *put these principles into action.*

Mindset

Is it this easy? Are you willing to consider an alternative to the grind? Are you willing to set aside doubt and disbelief long enough to give it an honest try?

Actually, because the motive power of what we're talking about here most certainly comes from the *subconscious*, I sometimes prefer to call it *heartset*. However, *mindset* seems to be more acceptable.

The law is: *See it first.*

You see, what happens to most people is that they get surrounded by limiting circumstances and take them to be the horizon of the world. In fact, they're nothing but a particular set of circumstances surrounding an individual at one particular time.

Lo and behold!... If they would move, the horizon would *change!*

Most people are not open to new ideas. Most people, for instance, cannot believe success can be so easy. Statistics tell us that 90% of the people who buy any book never read past the 1st chapter. Perhaps when they read about making $3,288 in a single hour, that's the ridiculous point they'll feel justified in laying this book down. ...dooming themselves to blunder along in the same dark and favorless rut they're already tired of struggling in.

Whereas, if, rather than being convinced it must be difficult – *SELF*-sabotaged from even trying! – they would **believe that it _is_ _easy_, then they'd go to work looking for _solutions_**.

The answers would come; they always do.

Either way, you get what you think.

It's all about thinking differently... It's a *lot* more fun. And a *lot* more rewarding! ...Being rich and happy!

Price Pritchett opens his breakthrough book, *You²*, with "A True Story." He tells the story of a time when he's sitting in a quiet room in a peaceful inn nestled among the pines about an hour's drive out of Toronto. How can you enjoy life more?

Then he hears something... He focuses his vision, and sees a fly at the window.

An ordinary fly wants outside – to freedom, food, and, of course, the pleasures of good sex. Beating its wings at higher and higher velocity, bracing its head and neck like a bull, it pounds the glass pane again and again and again. Trying harder and harder. Even in its fatigue, it raises itself once more – again and again – and makes a valiant attack.

Pritchett comments:

> This little insect has staked its life on reaching its goal through raw effort and determination.
>
> This fly is doomed. It will die there on the windowsill.
>
> Across the room, ten steps away, the door is open. Ten seconds of flying time and this small creature could reach the outside world it seeks. With only a fraction of the effort now being wasted, it could be free of this self-imposed trap. The breakthrough possibility is there. It would be so easy.

A true story... And Pritchett intends that you understand he's talking metaphorically about you. You see it every day. Both partners working. Different hours. Two jobs – no insurance, no quality time, permanently fatigued. Guilt about how you're treating your children and your family – but you're pressed by your job.

Work A Few Hours A Day. There *is* an easier way. *Breakthrough!* They envy me... Working a few hours a day, most weekdays, that is... from home... 3 hour lunches... Entertaining at the best places in town... Vacations to California, Florida, Greece, Egypt, and Ecuador... Living in a 4 story home...

They can't quite figure me out... but they know, in one word, I enjoy something they only dream about – *independence!*

But I'm revealing it all to you! It's *mail order*. Specifically, "Mail Order" in the *Information Age*.

Everything that I share with you in this book, in my courses, in everything I say and do, you can do, too.

> *I'm a lot richer now than I was when I sat down to write an hour ago. My $3,288.90 for an hour's worth of hanging out is greater than a month's take-home pay for millions of "successful" Americans!*
> – Ted Ciuba

I'm a lot richer now...

If you will. Just like the fly. That's what stops most people, you know, not "ability." The fly had the "ability" to fly out the open door.

Your job is wearing you out, stealing the best of your life, to enrich *somebody* else!

I log onto the internet, and I've got hundreds or thousands of dollars worth of orders. I check my fax machine, and I've got hundreds or thousands of dollars worth of orders. I open my mail, I've got hundreds or thousands of dollars worth of orders. I pick up the phone when it rings, and I've got hundreds or thousands of dollars worth of orders.

I just kick back and smile while my bank balance grows every day, plan my next getaway, and talk marketing with people all over the world. You can too!

My consulting practice has grown into an international business, with work in North America, Europe, the South Pacific, and the Latin World (¡Mi favorito!). Though I travel a good deal, all paid for by the client, most of this work is done over the phone, the fax, the internet, and with overnight delivery services, while I'm enjoying life with my family and friends in Nashville, Tennessee.

Start Working Easy! But none of it happened until I swore off working hard, quit my last job, and started *working easy*. The biggest hurdle you may have is *believing* it can and should be so easy! Just like the fly.

And that fly, and his approach to working harder for success? He dies. Beat up, wore out, on his back on the window sill. Pritchett tells the truth:

> "Trying harder" isn't necessarily the solution to achieving more. It may not offer any real promise for giving what you want out of life. Sometimes, in fact, *it's a big part of the problem.*

> If you stake your hopes for a breakthrough on trying harder than ever, you may kill your chances for success.

I invited Pritchett to tell you this story because it applies directly to you. "Mail Order" in the *Information Age* can make your life easy, prosperous, and productive! *Can't you just see it?!!*

Grab hold of that feeling and go for it!

Mail and *Grow Rich!*
$ ▲ ▼ ▲ $

## Chapter 2

Blowing The Lid Off
The World's Most Profitable Business

And why you should be selling "How-To" information *products.*

———— ◦•◦◉◦◦•◦ ————

How can I cruise the strip in Hollywood, California, feed llamas with my sweetie in the Andes of Perú, or go running on the beaches of Bermuda and still make *tens of thousands* of dollars?

How can I have the fax machine churning out orders all of the day and all of the night, each of them with eager instructions for me to debit someone's credit card and transfer the funds into MY bank account, ready for my immediate use? How can I bring an interested social friend into my office on New Year's Day, and just coincidentally, in the 5 minutes we happen to be in that little office (a spare bedroom in my home) – have a $782 order come faxing in? How can I make $3,288 an hour while I'm just hanging out? Most importantly – *how can you?!*

The "Mail Order" Metaphor

It's all possible because technology has advanced to the point that anyone willing to spend a few hundred dollars can have it all. Simple technology things like the fax. And the computer. And the phone. Your neighborhood Kinko's has several hundred thousands of dollars worth of equipment just waiting for your $25 order. And, of course, we still have the old reliable pony express. But, when you want it, you've got overnight delivery and wire transfers. There's been a revolution, and <u>you</u> <u>are</u> <u>the</u> <u>beneficiary</u>! You now have *everything* that a giant multinational conglomerate has.

But what all this really says is that it's not "just" *MAIL* today. You know, that's how it got started. People received a Sears Roebuck or Montgomery Ward catalog in the mail, sent their order in through the mail, and received their order through the mail. It's still a great treat to receive merchandise through the mail, isn't it? <u>Everyone</u> <u>loves</u> <u>it</u>!

However, though it remains an integral component of the **direct response** business, the communications channels have expanded *way* beyond the pony express. Back then, at the beginning of this century, mail was all there was.

Today, "mail" no longer plays the preferred role. We still use the term "mail order," but it is a metaphor for the mediums of **direct response** marketing and fulfillment.

> You say you don't accept credit cards?! Some people think this is a problem. Well, I'll tell you what... I'll *give* you guaranteed sources that *will* accept and process your credit card orders. No matter *who* you are... Even if your credit bureau report is a *disaster! Continue reading* to see how I've completely obliterated that problem for

And, by the way, mail is *still* a very big component of the mail order business. For the majority of direct response businesses it still carries the operational onus of the business. (Internet based companies being the significant exclusion, much to their cost-saving benefit!) A look at the mail that enters your house any week will amply testify to that.

But you can go the other way, too, 100% online. That's mail order, too. There are more and more businesses opening up every day that operate *solely* online. Of course there's the obvious ones like Amazon.com, but there's already hundreds of thousands of solely online businesses. Kirt Christensen has started 4 online businesses in the last couple of years, every one of them 100% online. He recently sold one of them for $11 million dollars. Corey Rudl, a "little guy" internet success legend, has made over $5.4 Million with his computer set up in his garage.

But even these successes can be called child's play, if you know anything about what's happened in the stock market with internet stocks. It's becoming routine to hear about some kid going from a net worth of 6 pizza coupons to $500 million in 18 months. *Online*. It's thrilling!

Yes, "mail" order has expanded. In today's information age, it is multi-dimensional. So what *mail order* comes to mean is direct *marketing* using any or all of the means available, commensurate with your resources and ambitions. The mail, the phone, the fax, the internet, courier services, wire transfers... You're not limited as to how you put the word out, and you're not limited as to how you take the money in! Nor are you limited in delivery options today.

Direct response marketing is essentially a form of marketing wherein advertisements, publicity, web sites, email, and, yes, regular mail, whichever is used, all solicit the order directly from the ad. It's the famous "not available in bookstores" line – it's not! You order it from the TV 800#, prompted by a commercial of some sort, or from the radio, or a magazine ad, or from reading an exciting letter that really pounds on all your hot buttons....

Even though mail does much of the work, it's just a component channel. For instance, Columbia Record Club runs an ad... You can respond by mail, fax, phone, or on the internet. *That's* what you want – *ease of ordering*.

Your product may be *delivered* by mail – but fewer and fewer people are taking the time today to write a check and *mail* it in. Instead, they use their credit card. On the phone. Or, today, more and more people go to the fax or the computer. Most people with discretionary income today have a fax and a computer. (And if your prospects don't have discretionary income, you'll go broke!) Millions more join the internet revolution every month!

What's so different today from the olden days, is that everything in business today is readily accessible by anybody! By printing letters on your computer, by building a simple website, and by putting a professional sounding message on your answering machine, you have the ability to create the same *appearance* as a giant multinational corporation!

Now, don't get me wrong, you *can* get started with nothing but a phone and the mail... In fact, some people *only* accept orders by mail, as their way of doing business. These people simply want a low-key income with no hassles. But an ambitious marketer would ask, "Why not let people send me money however they like?"

And even if you start with nothing but a phone and the mail, surely, once the money starts pouring in, you'll want to get a fax and computer. (Not that you yourself ever have to figure out how to actually use them.) It just makes your reach and your profitability so automatic, so easy, so **L-A-R-G-E**, and so *OUTRAGEOUSLY FUN!!!*

Phone, fax, internet, mail... It all works.

You say you don't accept credit cards?! Some people think this is a problem. You sales can *easily* double when you do! Well, I'll tell you what... I'll *give* you guaranteed sources that *will* accept and process your credit card orders. No matter *who* you are. They're called *fulfillment centers* and *order-taking services*. You can find them in the yellow pages of any big city. Try out Mountain West Communications at 1-800-642-9378. 24 hours a day they'll take your orders, process the credit cards, and send you the money!

Makes mail order easy!

If you want to accept and process credit cards yourself, surf up to the "Resources" page at http://www.mailandgrowrich.com   There you'll find links to several of the best merchant processors. The merchant arena is as volatile as the *internet* itself, but we'll always have the best 2-3 sources for you there. Look for reliability, a low discount rate, real-time internet processing, and *shopping cart* compatibility (for your web sales). To stay advised of the *latest* merchant breakthroughs, cyber up to the web site.

The Advantages of Not [Only] Mail Order

It's good that this business isn't just done by mail. You'll learn to love this fact. From our point of view, the fax, the phone, and the internet are all better! You're asking your customer to do less work, which means he or she is more likely to order from you. Additionally, you get the transaction completed immediately, which money in *your* account definitely brings a flush of satisfaction.

Mail is slow and puts more distance between the transacting parties. It's burdensome to write a check, find a stamp, and mail it in. Plus – and your consumers all know this – it means the product delivery will be slowed by 3-7 days. *Not what they want!* The phone, fax, and email collapse that distance. It's truly a "High Tech, High Touch" world. Customers want the assurance of personal attention when they want it. You can give it to them!

How you get the majority of your orders depends on your marketing approach. For example, in this comparison between the figures of Australian Peter Sun, a new light among successful marketers, and ours, you can see that we market extensively on the internet. Sun doesn't have a web site, does he?

Sun	**Parthenon**
85% telephone	45% phone
10% fax	35% internet
5% mail	15% fax
	5% mail

What you surely see in both cases, is the relative un-importance of mail in today's market. 5% of the business, in either case. Yet it's still called mail order. It's a metaphor. It's romantic to talk about it, because it still represents the *physical* asset called *cash*.

Today we even call TV and radio "conventional" medium.

Yes, today, the *internet* is hotter than ever! If you're especially interested in making your fortune on the internet, stay tuned... You'll be glad you did.

The Surprisingly Small Math To A Million Dollars

Most people I run across think you have to have a blockbuster seller to make tons of money. *Wrong!* The media has us thinking that way. But what if you would like to earn a million dollars? Do you know it takes only 50,075 copies of a $19.97 book to earn a million dollars?

And what if you wrote *1001 Ways To Be Romantic*, like Greg Godek, and sold 1,000,000 copies at $19.95. How about a sizzling **$19,950,000!?!**

$19,950,000!!

There's one more math step I'd like to take you through. When you sell 50,075 units of a book at $19.97, how much do you actually get to *keep*?

What if, after all marketing, production, and fulfillment costs – all the costs of your business – you only get to keep 50% of that? **$499,998.88**. Not too shabby for a few hours work, is it?

And if you sell a million *units*, you only get to keep $9.9 Million!

See It For Yourself!

The Surprisingly Small Math To A Million Dollars

Units	Price	To Earn...
50,075	$19.97	$1,000,000
25,019	$39.97	$1,000,000
10,309	$97.00	$1,000,000
3,367	$297.00	$1,000,000
1,357	$737.00	$1,000,000
696	$1,437.00	$1,000,000
358	$2,797.00	$1,000,000

Reality Chicklet   **"It's Your Turn!"**

Try a few price points of your own

Formula:

To Earn	divided by	Price Point	=	Units Required
$1,000,000	[example]	$29.97		33,367
$1,000,000				
$1,000,000				
$1,000,000				

The point is that your involvement can be minimal, yet *in mail order* you can be raking in the money. *It's not that hard to sell 10,309 courses at $97 – on any subject*! And pocket a cool million dollars.

Just get started!

Literally! Money comes in all hours of the day and night! Phone. Fax. Email. Only the mail is predictable. Monday through Saturday.

Hey, life is great! I wouldn't want it any other way!

You too can start humbly. You too can be successful. Just follow the simple instructions in *Mail and Grow Rich*, and *YOU* too *will* be successful!

Ted Nicholas started with a $97 ad. He was an ordinary guy one day, an apparent failure – deeply in debt and worried about survival. A few days later he was getting *bags* of mail from the post office every day at his house, filled with orders – with beautiful cash, checks, and money orders! He pulled in $400,000 in 4 months. Over $500 *Million* in his career of some 20+ years.

Gary Halbert got the electricity turned back on, wrote a 1-page letter, and borrowed a first class stamp. That project has earned over $1 Billion to date! Gary routinely spins out million dollar projects today.

Cindy Cashman wrote and self-published a book under an assumed name. While most publishing house "authors" are grateful for a single purchase, Cindy never sold a single book. She sold *Everything Men Know About Women*, by Dr. Alan Francis, only by the case lot, 100 books at a time! Her book was absolutely blank – nothing but a cover and 128 blank pages. Talk about *leveraging* information! Now she's retired with her million dollars to the posh side of Lake Travis in Austin, Texas. I first met the charming lady when she was vacationing in Bermuda.

Russ von Hoelscher is a mail order icon. He was visiting with 2 friends 1 summer weekend, sharing what he knew about mail order. The recorders were running all the while. They edited them into 8 hours of cassettes and offered them by mail order. They sold 6,743 sets of the "Program," for a total of $1,314,885. (6,743 x $195 = $1,314,885. See how easily the "Math To A Million Dollars" multiplies out?!!) **P.S.** That's off only *one* "information product" in his catalogue!!! Russ says it – ***"We took in an average of $25,286.25 a week!"***

Ted Ciuba started with a free classified on *America Online*. Today he runs a worldwide multi-million dollar consulting and direct response company giving aspiring millionaires and business people the *information, resources, motivation,* and *assistance* to easily and almost instantly capture their own million dollar goals.

Mark Nolan let the tape recorder run when he was giving a talk. A typist transcribed it, and he called it a book. Next he writes and mails a 4-page letter. Sitting at his kitchen table, he's sold more than $3,000,000 worth of that book.

Dave Ramsey hopelessly screwed up his financial life. Then he hit upon *Information Marketing*. Today he's a millionaire several times over, selling people advice on how to get out of or avoid financial trouble. Seminars, books, tapes, radio, franchises.

Peter Sun had a job delivering hot buns from the bakery – by bicycle! He scraped up a few bucks from tips, ran a small ad, and the response swelled till, in a few months he was earning $10,000 per week! He quit his lousy delivery boy job...

"Earning More Money In A Week Than Before In A Whole Year!"

Robert Allen is fond of saying, "You Are One Classified Ad Away From A Fortune!" He knows whereof he speaks. One day he placed a cheap classified ad in his local paper – costing less than $20. His phone went berserk, and within weeks he was earning $10,000 a DAY in the information business, pulling down six figures a *month*!

Eileen & T.J. Rohleder of Goessel, Kansas, sent off thousands of dollars – for one business opportunity after another. Most were based solely on theory, and lacked key processes to make them practical. Some were outright scams. Many the nights they labored. Then they came up with an original way to use classifieds and the telephone to sell. No more carpet cleaning for the Rohleders! *Success FLOODED in!*

> This business made us rich. *Just 4 years after we started* we had taken in a total of over $10-million dollars. Our lives

were changed forever. All our dreams came true. We bought new homes, cars, and great vacations. We gave money to our family and did all the things we used to dream about.

Success brings a certain change... People respect you more... They look up to you... You're an expert, a guru, a respected person... If you've earned a lifetime's worth of cash in a few months, you're suddenly no longer "normal." Even though you were perfectly normal 6 months earlier when you were still struggling...

Which is exactly my point. All these people are "normal." They may appear bigger than life today – but it's just the glow of success. Of course, they've each learned a lot and can maintain and repeat the performance. But, though they have more success and connections today, there was a day when there was NO DIFFERENCE between where you are now and where you want to be.

A lifetime's worth of cash in a few months. How would you like to go into your job with a $400,000 bank account and quote Johnny Paycheck?:

"Take this job and *shove it!*"

The More You Mail The More You Make

And, you say you want more money?!.. *The more you mail the more you make!*

What's holding you back?

Let's look at the mechanics of a real life mailing of a 1,000 pieces. Your first effort doesn't have to be like this example below, but, after you've been at it awhile, you'll probably think this is a relatively small first effort. Assume a mere 7% response rate, quite legitimate for a $39.97 + $7.00 s/h = $46.97 book to a targeted audience. Of course, you're going to have some expenses.

Test Mailing

Pieces	1,000.00
Printing	$277.00
Stuffing	$40.00
Postage	$320.00

List		$185.00
Cost to mail		$822.00
Evaluation		
Cost per letter		$0.82
Number letters		1000
Response rate		7.00%
Number of purchases		70
Amount of purchase		$46.97
Gross Income		$3,287.90
Expenses		
Mailing		$822.00
Product Cost	$3.00	$210.00
Fulfillment	$3.00	$210.00
Overhead & Returns	$3.00	$210.00
Total Expenses		$1,452.00
Total Profit		**$1,835.90**
Total profit per book		**$26.23**
Total profit per letter		**$1.84**

After all the shooting's over, you've made $1,835.90. That's $26.23 per book sold, or $1.84 per letter actually mailed.

Okay, $1.84 per letter mailed may not sound like too much... Even though you made $1,835.90 on the whole package. Even though *you* didn't really do anything. This profit includes having someone else do ALL the shipping and handling.

Sure, the first time you go through the process, it can seem somewhat complex. But after you've done it a few times – had your learning curve and got relationships set up – it's just a matter of making a few phone calls.

But, you see, the real beauty comes on the rollout. Up to now you've just sampled the waters...

You Get Rich On The Rollout!

Here's where it gets *really* sweet! **Put the leverage of mail order to work for you! Want More Money? Simple, mail more mail!**

Think this over for a moment. If every time you mail out a letter you make $1.84, don't you think that's pretty easy money? If you want to earn $1,000,000, simply make a few phone calls and direct that 543,478 letters be mailed out.

But there's more! Here's where you really appreciate the business control you get from direct mail! Strap yourself in, because you're about to go crazy with excitement, and I don't want you to get hurt!. **We're breaking out the *Multiplication Tables!***

When you roll out, the picture changes. There's lots of things working together for you on the rollout! Let's say because of your headline, bonus, warranty, and price tests, you've been able to raise the response rate from 7% to 9.85%, while simultaneously increasing the package price from $39.97 + $7.00 s/h = $46.97 to $47.00 + 7.00 s/h = $54.00, again confirmed by a few more introductory test mailings. Also, because you're now a bulk customer, your price per direct mail letter drops slightly from 82¢ to 68¢, and your product production cost drops from $3.00 each to $2.38 each. These are realistic figures.

> *Mail order allows business owners to tirelessly, relentlessly, and inexpensively make their best, most compelling, most powerful cases without ever deviating from their rehearsed sales pitch, without ever getting cold feet, without ever forgetting an important point, without ever flinching when a customer gives them a difficult retort, countering every objection, and delivering the perfect close.*
> – Jay Abraham

Indeed, let's *see!*

Cost per letter	$0.68
Number letters	1000
Response rate	9.85%
Number of purchases	98.5
Amount of purchase	$54.00
Gross Income	$5,319.00

Expenses		
Mailing		$680.00
Product Cost	$2.38	$234.43
Fulfillment	$3.00	$295.50
Overhead & Returns	$3.00	$295.50
Total Expenses		$1,505.43

Total Profit	**$3,813.57**
Total profit per book	**$38.72**
Total profit per letter	**$3.81**

Also, remember, your hard work is all done. You've got your product and copy in place. Now you just kick back with no work and no effort!

On the rollout you're earning $3.81 for every single letter that you mail out!!! That's with the *same* effort and risk. No more. Your earnings are up from $1,835.90 to $3,813.57, a very *doable* 108% increase!

And you're no fool! How long do you think it would take you to ask this question?:

"How many names can I <u>mail to</u>?"

Grab hold of this one! Direct marketing is not a crapshoot! Once your project is producing profits, you simply roll out on success. The numbers get larger. It's that simple. Also, in this populous country of ours, there's hardly a category that doesn't have 1,000,000 or more names.

$$1,000,000 \times \$3.81/\text{ltr} = \mathbf{\$3,810,000}$$

Wowee! *Multiplication was never this fun in school!*

> *Since you have to think anyway, you might as well think big.*
> – Donald Trump

But wait! Let's do a little more math, trying on a few different sets of the "universe" of names for people interested in your product. Let's say, averaging the effects of dilution (reaching to people beyond the first levels of predisposed interest in your product) and duplication (same names on different lists), your response rate takes a staggering drop of 40% down to a 5.91 response rate. That would bring your profit per letter down to a meager $2.02 per letter mailed. Everything else remains the same, of course, as it has been tested to be effective. Let's see...

Names	1,000,000	2,000,000	5,000,000
Profit/Letter	$2.02	$2.02	$2.02
Total Profit	**$2,020,000.00**	**$4,040,000.00**	**$10,100,000.00**

How would you like to make $2,020,000 in a couple of years?

The good news is <u>you</u> <u>can</u>!

Starting from ground zero, you could easily do this inside of a couple of years in "mail order"!

Reality Chicklet. What if you'd done a mailout of a 1,000 letters and lost money? How much? The likelihood of a *zero* return is almost infinitesimal... especially if you're following a good salesletter checklist! It's only when you've got the numbers that you launch yourself into a rollout.

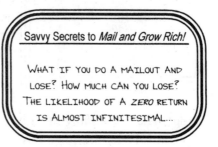

Savvy Secrets to *Mail and Grow Rich!*

WHAT IF YOU DO A MAILOUT AND LOSE? HOW MUCH CAN YOU LOSE? THE LIKELIHOOD OF A *ZERO* RETURN IS ALMOST INFINITESIMAL...

So, you can lose *some* money... but not very much. Then, of course, it's made up for with the winners.

It's Not a Crapshoot, But *It Is A NUMBERS Game!*...

The big event is to get a definitive win in an optimized test marketing effort, and then roll out with the winner!

If you have a stinker... two things: first, you probably made back some or *most* of your money... so it wasn't a washout. You're not gambling like that. You've also received feedback on what's *not* successful. Proceed as the market indicates, testing something *different*, such as a different headline, a higher or a *lower* price, a different offer, or a different guarantee.

This is *optimization* – getting the highest return possible out of every dollar you invest, out of every ad you run, out of every process you employ. Place two ads side-by-side. Nine times out of ten, there will be a significant difference in pulling power, attributable to headline, offer, bonus, premise, or a group of other things, which I promise to discuss with you in greater depth.

Optimization is essentially a scientific process wherein we test, or try out, different alternatives to find the better one. We can't tell by guessing, even by "educated guesses." But the marketplace will always reveal its preferences.

> *When you test something and you know you have a winner –*
> *there's no risk involved!*
> – E. Joseph Cossman

So your business becomes, in effect, an arena of science. You don't risk very much. But trying a few alternatives will usually give you one that far outperforms the others... That's the one you rollout with!

This is every business person's dream... And you've got it in mail order. There's *nothing* like it! To have definable, knowable profits!... To control and eliminate risk!

Because, when the numbers are secure, it's like you're playing with a **rigged table**... Of course you're *winning!!!*

...And *the best is yet to come!* So far, you haven't seen anything but the *beginning!* I can't wait to show you how you can pyramid your profits to over $100,000 from a single customer – starting with just a $337 sale!

Mail and *Grow Rich!*
$ ▼ ▲ ▼ $

## Chapter 3

Information Marketing

There are two distinct aspects to business. If you understand this distinction, you'll be light years ahead of 95% of your competitors...

Most people do it wrong... poor product, low prices, ineffective advertising, traditional opportunity... No wonder they fail!

You won't have to do that.

> *Every business is first and foremost a marketing vehicle.*
> *Only after you understand that does your brilliant and badly needed product stand a chance in today's competitive marketplace.*
> – Ted Ciuba

Most people don't understand the rudimentary division in business between the *two* prime divisions of business – any business.

Every business consists of the **core expertise** – that is, the product or service that is offered. However, many people stop there, thinking they're in the design business, or consulting business, or landscaping business, or oil business, or railroad business, or dance business... At best, they've only got half the picture.

The *real* business that every business person is in is the ***marketing business***. Cars, insurance, information products, etc... these are the particular "vehicles" each separate "business" chooses to do business *with*. That is, one person or company chooses to originate mortgages (vehicle) as their method to make money (the common end of all business). Another person or company chooses to sell antique furniture and trinkets (vehicle) as their method to make money (business).

Every business – *all* business – Is MARKETING. Without marketing, you have no productive activity. There is no income. There's just a product in a warehouse or a garage, or a skill lodged with an individual or a firm.

Most people don't understand this simple distinction. Your business is not really "health products," or "business opportunities," or "mortgages," or a "search engine submission service," or "indigenous products from Bolivia, or Civil War artifacts. Your business is really letting the people that might be interested in these products know that you have them, at a high value, and they can make their lives immediately better when they get them. *That's* marketing!

> *Whatever else you do, you are also in the marketing business.*
> – Jay Conrad Levinson

One easy way to sprint ahead of your competitors is to simply realize that you're in the *marketing* business. Leave 'em eating your dust!

To Optimize... To fully optimize your results, you should take your understanding to the next level. You'll more fully optimize when you conceive both your product and marketing maneuvers as including substantial elements of each other, simultaneously affecting and being affected by each other. Independent and integrally connected.

> *To thrive in business, you must be able to market whatever it is you have to offer. Which means that regardless of whatever business you may think you're in, you are also in a marketing business.*
> – Bob Serling

Fortunately, it *sounds* a lot worse than it is... In theory you might think you need to be versed in Eastern mysticism. In practice I'm just talking about *reverse engineering*. The most successful enterprises are those that select their market first, according to where they find a *starving crowd* and *then* adopt and develop their product with an eye to what that market *wants*. After having decided on your product, you then develop and launch your marketing plan with your market and your product both clearly in mind. Talk about *targeting!*

Easy. There's only 3 things. Market, product, marketing. Easy. When you know how!

WHEN you know the secrets, it's a breeze. Kind of like the juggler, keeping 5 balls in the air... *Easy*, when you know the secrets. Then it's just developing the flow that comes with mindful and engaged experience.

We Have A Very Strong Bias...

You and I... We want the *business* that offers us the most advantages with the least disadvantages, don't we? Maximum returns for minimum effort. Right?

Maximum money in minimum time.

That's why you need to know about *Information Marketing*. That's what we call the *direct response marketing* of *information products*. When you combine the advantages of direct response marketing and information products together in *Information Marketing* you've just found the best business there is!

It's trouble-free, *profitable*, and reliable.

There is no more ideal product than an information product. In a nutshell, it's got a high perceived value, it's cheap to reproduce, and very affordable to ship. Losses due to damages are virtually non-existent. Your prospects are easy to find, cheap to approach, and easy to convert.

All of these things make a *setup* for the perfect business... Which is what *Mail and Grow Rich* is all about!

Successful, Savvy, in tune with the trends...

Using Today's Simple Technology Tools Like The Phone, A Fax, Your Computer, And The Neighborhood Copy Machine, Working Part-Time From Your Home, You Can Quickly, Easily, Safely, and Insanely Earn *Well Over $100,000 Per Year* in...

"Mail Order" in the *Information Age!*

No need for employees, expensive overhead... You can live your life on the beachfront, if you want. Or from home in Spokane, working part-time, if that's where you want to live.

Announcing!
- The "Marketing" of "Information Marketing" -
Direct Response – The Greatest Method

Direct response marketing, or "mail order" is a *method* – 1 way – of conducting the marketing and selling function of your business. There are many more, such as opening a storefront and letting people walk in, or sending a sales force out to make calls, but mail order is the most elegant, trouble free, affordable, and profitable.

The principles of direct response marketing can be used to sell darn near *anything!* Just think of your own experience as a consumer and as a person who's seen lots of ads in magazines, newspapers, the radio, and on TV. (Among other places.)

Companies are using direct mail to successfully sell furniture, magazines, gourmet food, jewelry, fine wine, electronics, kitchen ware, clothing, toys, magazines, cigars, records, golf equipment, home loans, business opportunities, insurance, credit cards, computers, software, adult things, works of art, shoes, vitamins, cameras, office supplies, printing, wigs, flowers, gardening plants and equipment, books, cosmetics, videos, exercise equipment, real estate, real estate plans, pet supplies, collectibles, newsletters, and much more!

Think there's any opportunity in mail order? Nobody's have become millionaires overnight. The *first* successful letter that Gary Halbert wrote has already pulled in over $700 *million!* (Using conservative estimates... others place it 3-4 times as high!) He wrote it one evening after they turned the electricity back on in his house!

It's Easy To Find Your Market

We affectionately call Gary Halbert the "wildman" of the copywriting profession. He once asked a group of aspiring marketers a simple question. "Assuming," he says, "you've got a hamburger stand..." He continued, "and you could have any *one* feature concerning your business... What would it be?"

The motivated group shouted their answers:

"Killer advertising!"
"The best location!"
"Reliable help!"
"The best hamburger around!"
"A price lower than my competitor's!"
"The cheapest price!"

And so it went... After all the answers were out, and he'd written them all on the board, he asked everybody to review the list, to think again... "Are you sure there isn't something else? If you can only have *one* thing?"

A few more things were mentioned, actually repeats or variations of things already on the board.

Then Gary, getting close, huddled with the crowd and whispered into the mic, "If I could only have ONE thing, I'd want...

"A Starving Crowd!"

Instantly everybody knew Gary was right.

With a starving crowd you don't need any advertising, any location will do, because they're there, and they're *hungry*. They're *MOTIVATED TO BUY!*

And if it takes a few minutes longer to get their burger, because you're short one unreliable employee, they'll wait. And nobody asks if you're the "best" burger around...

By the way, I've *never* met anyone over 12 years old who actually thought McDonald's had the "best" burger around... Have you? Of course, you know, no one sells *more!* **This should illustrate to you that it's more then just the "best" burger** that makes for financial success.

And, when a person's hungry, and you're the one there, you're not compared against some competitor's pricing, because there are no competitors... (For this reason you want to develop your *U.S.P.* – Unique Selling Proposition. *More on eliminating competition* later.)

And how's this for a sweet note?! With all these advantages, you'd be a fool to give your customers the "lowest" price and not make any money for yourself... And likewise not be around to serve them another day...

Things are totally different when you're selling to someone who's *aggressively seeking you out!* If you've ever been a salesperson, you know what a dream this is!

Well guess what? It's not a dream in mail order!

The advantages that you have with direct marketing allow you to target niche audiences. You only spend your advertising dollars in areas where you *know* people are *predisposed* to your product or service. People who are *hungry* to buy from you!

Different people read different magazines. When you advertise in different publications you are advertising to people with a *professed* interest in the subject matter. Everything from *The Economist* to *The Globe, The Wall Street Journal* to *People*, the *Hog Farmer's Update* to *Guitar Player, Vintage Porcelain Dolls* to *Sniper.*

Thus, if you have a dazzling new guitar wah-wah peddle, you don't waste your resources advertising it in *The Wall Street Journal*, do you? Few guitar players read *The Wall Street Journal*. But they do congregate in the pages of *Guitar Player*, don't they? Here's your *starving crowd!*

The same thing goes, in reverse, if you have a businessman's product. Sure, *some* guitar players are businessmen, with businessman's concerns... But, statistically very few pickers are businessmen. Therefore, you wouldn't waste your money on an ad for a businessman's product in *Guitar Player*. But *The Wall Street Journal* for a businessman's product? There's your *starving crowd!*

And with either publication you wouldn't advertise a great new high protein, high body building hog supplement, that would increase hog farmers' yields by 23.9%, would you? But if you're in the *Hog Farmer's Update*... There's your *starving crowd!*

Thus you see how niching goes. "Everybody" is *not* your customer. You're always seeking to optimize the value of your investment, so you only pay to reach people who are *predisposed* with an interest in your product.

Your costs are lower, your prospects are more responsive. And the money you make is multiplied many times over. It's easy to "Get rich in a niche." It's likely you'll go broke trying to sell to "everybody"!

Whether by advertisements in publications, or whether you rent mailing lists of proven mail order buyers *of similar products*, with direct marketing you approach your <u>exact</u>, <u>specific</u> <u>market</u>. It don't get no better than this!

It's like shooting fish in a barrel! They're there, gathered together in a little area, and you've got them.

It's entirely legal and ethical! Understanding how direct marketing works literally gives you a <u>license</u> <u>to</u> <u>print</u> <u>money</u>.

Who Should Use Direct Marketing?

Some people have the mistaken notion that direct marketing is only for "mail order" companies. You already know better. Nothing could be further from the truth.

Direct response is truly the *only* kind of advertising that any company should ever do. It's about maximizing your revenues! Minimizing your expenses. It's trackable. It stimulates *sales*. Conventional advertising doesn't work. It's not trackable. Why would you want to ever do anything else other than direct response advertising?

To maximize its effectiveness, even your yellow pages ad should be direct response oriented. Not only will you make more money – because you'll have an offer that inspires action, but you'll *know whether or not your ad is working*. You see, every time people ask for the unique special you've identified in your ad, you know they've seen it in the yellow pages.

Direct marketing brings a bundle of *particular* benefits to <u>any</u> <u>business</u> <u>in</u> <u>the</u> <u>world</u>!

Mortgage professionals, dentists, chiropractors, lawn care professionals, hair dressers, computer programmers, publishers, manufacturers, software developers, restaurants, consultants, speakers, printers, salespeople, nutritional companies, and almost any other business you can think of all use direct mail to generate leads and customers like mad. Watch your mail... or email.

Direct marketing offers you the ultimate in marketing firepower – ALL your money goes to *effective* marketing... with no waste on people who could never buy. *Hm-m-m-m.*

Ads And The Mail

The basic selling devices of direct response marketing are *ads* and the *mail*. You've no doubt seen millions of impressions, so you know what I'm talking about. Something you may not be aware of, however, is the 2 standard approaches these devices use.

Lead Generation and Direct Selling

For all the exciting facts simply request your...

FREE Special Report!

2-Step Selling

Any ad or sales letter approaches the selling effort either with 1-step or 2-step selling. Lead generation, or 2-step selling, refers to the process of getting an interested person to respond at a low level of involvement, and then stepping them up to the intended sale.

Any time you read, watch, or hear an ad that invites you to respond for a "free special report" (a <u>very</u> <u>powerful</u> sequence of words!), or "free information," you're seeing *2-step advertising* in action.

When they request it, they've taken step one in this sequence.

The free special report arrives, all right, and it's loaded with valuable information. Its sole purpose, however, is to get you to buy the product or service being offered. Some marketers refer to it as a "disguised" sales letter. It is.

When they order the product, they've taken step 2.

Direct selling, or 1-step selling, most frequently involves mailing a full sales package to a prospect with your first contact. In fact, however, any ad that asks you to send money is a 1-step ad. Thus, for instance, you see many advertisements in magazines, papers, and the TV that ask you to send anywhere from $3 to $79 dollars to purchase the product. That's 1-step, selling directly from the ad.

Even with affordable products, but especially with more expensive products, it's easier to capture the sale with 2-step selling. That's why I'd recommend that anyone start with 2-step marketing.

A more sophisticated approach actually combines *both* approaches. For instance, an ad or mail piece might 1-step you into a $19.97 book, which might in turn, even while delivering full value for your purchase, invite you to get involved with a bigger, more benefit-laden course on the subject or opportunity. Thus you've got a 1-step ad, with the product itself working as a 2-step special report.

Publicity Can Make You $1,000,000

Fame, riches, love, FUN, relationships, prestige, respect!...

It can all be yours... With a few press releases – literally, *with a few clicks of your left mouse button* – you're an instant expert, an authority on your topic or product. And, aren't you? Whatever it is you sell, you're the expert on it – compared with thousands and hundreds of thousands of others...

How about being a guest on radio talk shows... appearing on *Larry King?*...

TV... *Oprah, Donahue, Sally, The Today Show?*...

Newspapers... *The Washington Post, The New York Times, The San Francisco Chronicle?*...

Magazines like *Time, Forbes, Popular Mechanics?*...

Think it might boost your career?

One single piece of publicity in *Family Circle*, earned Harold Moe $3,591,000. Most people think Moe did okay.

Perhaps you've heard of Paul Hartunian, who offers simply the best entrepreneurial publicity course in existence today...... (Available from Parthenon Marketing.) He earned a smacking kool $400,000 for ½ hour's work. (At that rate it'd take him an hour and 15 minutes to earn $1,000,000!) We're *talking leverage here!*

> *Family Circle* featured the book of <u>self-published</u> <u>author</u>, Harold Moe, *How To Make Your Paycheck Last.*
>
> ➡️ That *SINGLE* piece of publicity brought in over *180,000 orders* at $19.95 each. Just in case you're wondering... that's –
>
> In 60 Days!
>
> ## $3,591,000!!!

That's not the greatest prize for a single press release, but most people would think that's pretty good for a man who woke up one morning to his radio alarm, got motivated by the news, ran to his word processor and compressed the guts of his inspiration into a few paragraphs. He became famous *and rich* as the man selling the Brooklyn Bridge.

<u>If</u> <u>you</u> <u>know</u> <u>*how*</u> <u>to</u> <u>use</u> <u>publicity, you can get rich off of it</u>. Most people don't.

If you try to *sell* – using the media for an advertisement – you'll be an *instant loser*. You'll only last the 3 seconds it takes to interject filler... On the other hand, if you get interviews and name and face recognition, and you don't make any money, you're also a loser. Fame without money is *not* acceptable. Fame *with* money is very good.

Fortunately, it's simple to convert yourself into a winner simply by understanding a few crucial things about publicity.

It all basically refers to treating the media as you would any marketing target – by giving them what they want – and collecting a *willingly paid* price for doing it.

So your solution is to offer the media *news*. That's what they want. And as part of that "news package" that you're giving them, is a mention of your contact information, an address or phone. It's a simple deal that the media knows.... The deal of the day. But you can only count on it if you ask for it.

It doesn't have to be a dream...

Easy, Instant, Cheap – Technology-Advantaged – Predictable, and <u>10</u> <u>Times</u> <u>More</u> <u>Powerful</u> <u>Than</u> *Paid* <u>Advertising</u>!!!

Here we are, face-to-face with the outrageous power now in the hands of the little guy – with homebased technology. Simple stuff, really. Like a computer with Win-Fax Pro... and a telephone line. You write a *guaranteed-winner* press release (because you know *how* to do it) in a few minutes. Then you fax-blast your press release to thousands of media sources with the click of your mouse.

Publicity gives it *ALL* to you! It's easy, instant, *cheap*, technology-advantaged, predictable, and *outrageously effective!!!* – 10 times more powerful than paid advertising!

Let's start with writing a release. Unlike a sales letter, which may run anywhere from 4 - 44 pages, a good press release is a <u>single</u> <u>page</u>. *Double-spaced!*

And, while writing a sales letter can be a mindbuster, to say the least, the standard press release consists of just 3 sections.

First, there's the "story," in which you summarize everything. Second, there's the "backup," in which you create credibility

> *A broadcast-faxed news release is what got me a TWO PAGE ARTICLE, IN COLOR, IN FORBES MAGAZINE.*
>
> *If I bought two pages of advertising in Forbes, I'd pay between $50,000 and $75,000.*
>
> *<u>I paid 15¢</u>.*
>
> *Which price do you like better: $75,000 or 15¢?*
>
> – Paul Hartunian

for the source. This can be as simple as... "according to Doug Dukes, who's ridden the rails now for 22 years..." Doug's story will now have credibility because he *IS* an authority on railroad hoboing. The third section is the concluding "close," where you go for the throat (excuse me, the "sale.")

Press release writing really is that easy. In fact, if you complicate it more than that, you're bound to suffer.

There's another thing you should know about in the newsrooms of America & the world. *A fax vibrates with urgency*. Mail – as you've evidenced by sending it through the system that takes *days* instead of *seconds* – can wait. Nothing to it... What's a few more weeks? (Not the way I want to run my publicity campaign!) Mail has become antiquated. It's *dated* before it crosses the newsroom portal, and it's treated that way.

If this little pinch of publicity has you yearning for more, don't go anywhere! More later.

The Simple Tools Of Direct Marketing

Believe it or not, we've already identified all the tools of direct marketing. They're as simple as advertising (whether classified or space ads), sales letters, publicity releases, the mail, the internet, the fax machine, and the telephone. (Telemarketing is one application of the telephone.) Any entrepreneurial-minded person has the ability to use all of these tools, easily.

Advertising and direct mail are the old reliable staples of direct marketing. They work. They work good. When you have a good product, and you have good copy, you just put these mediums to work, and they churn out money for you regularly.

Publicity can offer you financial and credibility rewards that dwarf the returns from paid advertising, and it can do it for literally pennies of the cost of ads!

Get Rich Quick On The Information SuperHighway

However, the *internet* is the hot new medium of direct response marketing. In fact, it's gotten to the point that 2 essential components of any well-addressed business include the *URL* and your email address. Without these items, you're looked at as a dinosaur. It sure happened fast... within a couple of years!

Fortunately, the same principles hold true on the internet as anywhere else. Offer a good product with good copy, making a good offer, and you'll get orders. The three things that are amazing about the internet are 1) how *cheap* it is! 2) the speed with which you can transact business! and 3) how great your reach is!

Truly, the internet and the worldwide web have gotten so cheap that there's really no excuse not to be on the web. And, by the way, email is now a great way to do your publicity campaigns, driving down the penny-pincher price of publicity to *zippo!*

And web space? Today, if you'll do a search on the internet under "free web space," you'll find acres of it! We also offer certain programs to put you on the web. We'll place you on the web, do all the work and programming for you, optimize your marketing programs, and send all the orders from your site directly to you! We'll make all the arrangements for processing your credit cards, so that you don't have any trouble at all! All you do it participate in the greatest revolution to ever hit the marketing world.

Simply request the *"Web Site"* info from our office. It's free.

But, cheap on the web doesn't equate with ineffective! When you run an ad, for instance, you've got a lag time of a few days to a few months before the ad comes out and you see results. Not necessarily so on the internet. We got our first inquiries for a $997 product we put up on our web site within 5 *minutes* of putting the offer up. It didn't cost a penny to put that on the web, either!

After exchanging email correspondence back and forth a few times – at *zero* cost – just 5 days after we'd placed the report online, we received our first order. It was an *international* order, from *Switzerland!* We would <u>never</u> have placed an ad in a single Swiss paper or magazine, but, on the web he searched us out and sent in his $997!

I can't imagine a better direct response vehicle than the worldwide web!

Also, the majority of people on the web have credit cards. Not only does a credit card make it more convenient to buy, this very convenience successfully encourages credit card holders to spend more money. Get a web site and let them spend that money with you!

The general consensus with web advertising is that you need to tone down the hype factor. Provide good solid information, and build a relationship.

Truly, it's my humble opinion that those who aren't looking at the web today are somewhat blind!!! Missing a great portion of the fortune they could have! But don't worry... If you're not going after it, somebody else will!

Announcing!
- The "Information" of "Information Marketing" -
Information – The Greatest Product

I want you to get rich. But I also want you to do it in the most rapid and trouble-free way there is. So, no, I'm not going to suggest you sell hamburgers... But I do want you to sell to a starving crowd... I want you to sell *information products!*

Believe me, there is no better product than a "how to" information product. Information products have a high perceived value, which makes them easy to sell – at high prices – which, of course, means your *profit$ are outrageous!*

Not only that... but, *take your pick!* Your opportunities to furnish information products are *unlimited!* Think about the millions of information subjects out there!... Everything from fly fishing to flight in covert operations... Tax compliance to tax avoidance to taxidermy and calling a taxi in Manhattan. Gaming to goldmining...

Pick your passion. Take your pick.

Also, the thing that eats most peoples' lunch, isn't hardly a factor for you: you don't need any <u>inventory</u>! This is another particular and recent benefit that business in the *information age* gives you! – the breakthrough of **publishing-on-demand** makes it possible for the little guy to get rich overnight! You can get started <u>without any inventory</u>! Then, when the orders come in, the products are *cheap* and *easy to produce.*

Definition Of An "Information Product"

But first!... I think I'm getting ahead of myself... "What," you certainly may be asking, "do you mean by 'information products.' *Books?*"

Here's where you part company forever with all the well-intentioned, conventionally bred, mis-profit-informed people of the world. *Books?* Well, *yes* and *no*. Books, as you see them in the bookstore, no. At least, not if that's *all* there is.

You can't make enough money on books for books' sake. But, used strategically, you can make a killing.

Through conventional bookstore channels, your profit on a book is minuscule. Believe me, even if you self publish, but distribute your book through conventional channels, your share is minuscule. Like $7 on a $20 book. Even at that, you've got to pay for advertising at every turn. Not to mention the cost of the book itself, which may be $2.00 - $3.50. Then there's other costs...

Authors don't make money. Publishers make little.

Of course, if you have a book that really takes off, if you're that one person in 2,000,000... you may end up with a $100,000 TOTAL profit. But, friend, I didn't write this book to tell you how to earn $100,000 on a book, but $100,000 or more every year!

By staying in control and selling by direct response methods, you can *net* $15.00 on that same book. *Then*, when you have a million seller, you've got **$15,000,000** in your pocket!

How You Really Make Money In Information Marketing

But that's only the beginning! What *you* want, and what will make you rich, year in year out, with niche sales, is *information products!* And just what are "information products"? Simple: books, reports, audio cassettes, videos, diskettes, CD-Rom's... This kind of thing...

But first, let's back up a bit...

There's more about books. The only time you'd want a "book," is when it is strategically positioned to do more for you than simply be a "book."

To illustrate this idea, as well as what we in the direct response "how to" industry mean when we talk about "information products," take this very book, *Mail and Grow Rich*, for an example.

The book sells for a mere pittance of its true worth... It's aimed first at ordinary folks who want to earn an independent, prosperous living. Secondly, it's aimed at every business person in the world – especially those interested in the New World Order of *E-Commerce*. It truly contains closely guarded secrets – such as this very one we're discussing now – that can literally make you, or any other person who reads and acts on it, millionaire rich.

However, as a $19.97 purchase, it's available to everyone who wants one. *Nobody* is priced out of the market. And, as a $19.97 product, it fits well within the bargain range that newspapers, newsletters, magazines, and TV talk shows like to offer to their readers... Especially since it's on a topic that appeals to so many people – making money from home, on the internet. So I've created a product that can get millions of dollars worth of *free* publicity.

And every interview can mean $100, $1,000, $10,000 or more. For *free*. Because you *always* have your toll free number published with all publicity. 1-877- *4-RICHES*.

When I do a Los Angeles radio show and get 507 orders in 45 minutes, I've packed in a cool $10,125 – of which $8,958.90 is *mine* to keep – profit after expenses. Not bad for an hour's work, ¿no?

But, as you may have already noticed, in this very book I offer my reader a number of *other products* that give them the ultimate tools they need to be *super*-successful! There's the course created in conjunction with this book, the *Mail and Grow Rich* System, as well as references to others, such as the publicity course we talked about earlier.

To use an analogy, let's say you're a teacher teaching on any subject. Let's pick one... *Mountain climbing!* Now, when I come to your free introductory class, or read your free special report, or buy your $19.97 book (all information products) because I heard you on a radio interview or read one of your ads, I find you're teaching me how to climb mountains. I find you sharing unselfishly with me, the benefits of your interests, experience, and expertise. Some of the glories of the sport, as well as some of the dangers I need to be aware of today. A little bit about training. Maybe you describe a tense trip up the face of the treacherous El Capitán, and get me fired up to challenge that same mountain in Yosemite National Park.

Now that I'm better educated, I'm rearing to go! You're the expert and kind friend who has provided me all this low cost, valuable information. Who am I going to go to when I need pants, a jacket, boots, a knife, a hand warmer, properly packed emergency food and water? How bout spikes and a hammer, ropes, pulleys, and safety gear? How about a club, where like-minded companions can meet? How about a newsletter describing 2-3 of the world's best spots for mountain climbing every month?

And do I care if you make a fair profit on the merchandise? *Just like anyone else would?* But *you're* my friend – you've demonstrated it beyond any doubt. I already know and trust you...

I'm coming to *you!*

That's the power of information products. To create a multiple buyer, a lifetime friend and purchaser. Remember, though I give many example of my own experience, these principle are universal, and they apply to whatever valid product in the world you're selling!

So, returning again to the products I might sell to people who read my book, *Mail and Grow Rich...* These additional products have a higher dollar value, of course. So if only 5% of those original publicity-won customers purchase an additional $500 from me within the next several months, I've made an additional $12,500! Add that to the original $9,985, and now I've made $22,485!

You know why I'm in information marketing! **$22,485 for an hour's work**!

Believe me. You're getting real *insiders' secrets*. This is *not* something I would share around the pastry table at a church affair, or something I'd share in conversation at a Belle Meade social event.... Or even at the racetrack over *cervezas* (that's *beer*, for you gringos). But, because I want *you*, as an entrepreneur and valued friend to know the truth, I share it freely with you.

What if you only work a few hours a week? $22,485 x 3 = $67,455.00. Entirely possible.

So here we are, back where we began. What are information products? Simple, they are reports, brochures, booklets, books, manuals, audio tapes, video tapes, diskettes, and CD's.

Market reports, books, audios, videos, diskettes, CD-ROM's to an *info* STARVING CROWD.

Your Simple Info Formula To Millionaire $uccess!

And, here we are again, in today's *information* age, these are all ridiculously easy to accomplish! You can learn to create and/or acquire information products of your own with just a few phone calls. It's *never* been easier than it is today! Later you'll read about "How To Get Your Own Million Dollar Product." It contains *full* details.

High Perceived Value

If Halbert is remembered for the "starving crowd," perhaps Ciuba will be remembered for the "info junkie." (I guess I should be ashamed of it.)

The starving crowd speaks to a *passion* that must be fulfilled... *Junkie* takes that hunger one step further... *Junkie* recognizes that every person in that crowd will again have a driving hunger to fulfill. *Tomorrow. Same place. Same time. Same great profits! Perhaps even more than once a day!*... Every person in the crowd will be hungry again in a few hours, all morality aside... The junkie needs a *recurring* and *ongoing* "fix."

But let's talk about *differences* now. Under normal circumstances, there's a big difference in "relative values." Everybody and his brother's selling "food." This drives prices down... To where it approaches the value of what the person could provide for himself or herself. I mean, people *can* prepare their lunch at home and bring it with them.

It's different with a junkie. A junkie *can't* do the alternative thing of "fixing" their own passion, be it sex, drugs, or rock-n-roll (lapsing back into my 60's roots). This *RAISES* the price *IMMENSELY* as well as providing for *ONGOING, REPEAT BUSINESS!*

You Can't Live With Yourself If You're On The Take

PAY ATTENTION! In this discussion of junkies and their passions, don't infer that I would ever recommend you do anything illegal. I am NOT recommending you do anything illegal, immoral, or deleterious to life, fame, or character. Your own or anybody else's. That would be the height of stupidity! And against everything I stand for.

My whole philosophy is about *enjoying* life and helping *you* enjoy life, too! The stupidest thing you could ever do is get involved with anything illegal, immoral, or destructive of your health, character, fame, or freedom – or of others.

When I talk about an "info junkie" it's a *metaphor* and *analogy* to *illustrate* certain things...

- The easiest thing to sell is *something people want.*

- The *best* thing to sell is something people want badly!...

- They're going to spend their money with someone... Why not some of it to prosper *you*?!

- If you're selling something that people want *over and over again*, that they can't get anywhere else, then you'll get *rich!*

- There are *millions* of *info junkies* – the *whole society* is an *info junkie* – to get you rich.

- Your profits will blast out the roof!

But you can't live with yourself, your wife, your children, or your God if you're on the *take*. Don't take my word for it! Just look around. Those who are take advantage of humanity's foibles never win in the long term.

I am talking about the distinctly moral phenomenon of making a substantial profit while *contributing* to humanity's development and well-being.

On the *give*, you enjoy the true riches of life. *More* than *just* material wealth... True riches in every dimension! It's *too easy* to be a contributor *enjoying* life to do anything else! And, my experience teaches me that's the only way you ever really enjoy the riches that these mail order techniques can lay in your hands...

"Someone Who Can't Resist Spending Big Chunks Of Money!"

What characterizes a junkie? What does this mean?

In the information marketer's eyes, an info junkie is someone who can't resist spending big chunks of money. Someone who consumes information, in their own topic of interest, be it fashion, web design, import/export, gourmet coffee, teaching skills, medical malpractice, or even something as mundane as rice (there's a whole rice industry, don't forget).

<u>These</u> <u>people</u> <u>have</u> <u>an</u> <u>insatiable</u> <u>need</u> <u>for</u> <u>more</u> <u>information</u>!

A junkie just can't get enough of your product... Except for only temporarily – and that's short-term.

And it's high priced!...

There's literally thousands of different fields of interest, but let's talk about the *business opportunity* junkie. I can talk freely about this addiction, because I've got it!

There's hardly a week goes by that I'm not sending off for reports, books, or courses of various values, from free to $1,000. Several times a year I go flying away to some high priced $2,500 - $10,000 seminar.

And I'm *supposed* to know all this already! And I do know more than 99.999% of the population at large, and 98.6% of other marketers... "But," I tell myself,

> ...if I learn only *one* little thing, *one* new distinction, *one* new technique... or if this speaker helps me see something I already know in a new way that stimulates a new action on my part... Or if I get the motivation to do something new or different...

> Then I'll make back *multiples* of what I've invested in this program.

And, of course... there *is* a reason why I would say this to myself... The reality of the matter is, it happens again and again and again!

Just like the rush and the reward the junkie gets from his drugs, I get the same thing from the information. I *do* experience a surge of ideas and activity. And *money*.

Another thing that characterizes a junkie, is that he needs to up the dosage to get the same kick.

Higher qualities, greater amount – $19.97 book, $497 course, $5,000 seminar.

That's what you want – someone who can't resist spending big chunks of money! *That* characterizes a junkie. When you can hit on a junkie crowd... your fortune is assured.

Like I said, I know this market...

I'm not a fisherman, or a cook, or a model railroader, or an ornament maker, or a chiropractor, an NLP practitioner, a language teacher, a Tarot reader, or an oboe player, a pediatrician, a mountain climber, or a Harley rider... But the same thing holds true in these markets, too. **One little distinction – to an info junkie – in his or her area of passion – is worth it all.**

P.S. I always think that as marketers, we are the *luckiest*, because, for us, those distinctions result in a greater *bottom line. YES!!*

But from collecting porcelain plates to walking on fire, you name it, there's people who can't get enough information!

Sewing, model trains, warfare, engineering, literature, hot rods, cultures, politics, investments, web development, sculpture, collectibles, precious gems... money-making opportunities... religion, charities, medical practitioners, C.P.A.'s....

We are all info junkies, because we all are interested in making our lives better. Somebody's involved in any interest area you can name – from survivalism to sophistication. And like a junkie – people will pay whatever they have to pay for information. *Then they'll clamor for even more, of a higher quality and a higher price!*

My question to you?...

Somebody Has To Supply The Info Junkies... Why Not You?

For every group of interests there are buyers... People want security, want to make money, want a good relationship, want to appear attractive to the opposite sex, want the latest edge in their sport... For your particular interests, why don't you become the seller?

Your Profit$ Are *Outrageous!*

In fact, to *outsiders*, the profits we make are nothing short of *obscene*. Even the oil companies don't do as well as you and I do. Believe me, you've got to be careful who you tell!

Let me give you a *TRUE* example of the outrageous markups we enjoy! In Diversified Resources, Inc., one of the companies I'm affiliated with, we sell the *Paper Profit$* Course. It's a course on buying and selling "cashflows" – mortgage payments, leases, annuities, judgements, lottery winnings, car, marine, and airplane notes.

> Question: *If you were going into direct marketing today and didn't have a product, and had no money, how would you start?*
>
> Answer: *What I would do is take an existing product that's out there – not create a new one – and figure out a way to market it on a direct basis... and do a test for as little as $600, testing 1,000 names. I'd pick a product that already has a proven track record.*
>   – Ted Nicholas

The course teaches people how they can make upwards of $1,000 per hour in the cashflow industry, easily over $10,000 per month. The "product" itself consists of a manual with 2 cassettes, a special report, and a cover page. Here's our actual costs:

Binder	$1.81
Printed Text	3.54
2 Cassettes	.72
1 Special Report	.10
1 "Thank You" Cover Page	.01
Total	**$6.18**

When you consider that people pay from $97 to $497 for these manuals, things really start looking good! At $97, we make a 1,470% markup. And when we sell a $497 manual, which we regularly do, that's a...

7,942% markup!

Try doing that in the stock market!

How is it possible to sell a manual for $497? Some people, you know, don't believe it can be done... But it can be done quite easily... In fact, after I strolled the 8 second commute from my breakfast room to my "office" (spare bedroom) this morning... in less than 10 minutes, 2 orders have come in. One for $152.00. The other for $997.00. Our most popular product is the full $737 *Paper Profit$* course.

Can you see why I'm such an advocate of a home-based information products mail order business?!!

P.S. If you'd like to enjoy the same type of prosperity, with the identical products we are doing it with... stay tuned. I'll share exactly how you can make it happen!

So, how is it possible to sell a manual for $497? By this point you already know, don't you? The city is Junkieville, in the land of Information Products. NO other product allows these kinds of margins!

But, a 7,942% markup!?? Here's the distinction...

You're selling a *map*... not the paper.

Maybe it's true that it only "costs" you $6.18 to put a course together. But, because of the *information* it contains, it's worth *FAR* more.

I could imagine, couldn't you? that a thinned paper napkin which had the route to a pirate's treasure drawn out on it could command a *very high price.*

It's the *perceived value* thing all over again... You're *not* selling the cost of manufacture of the "product," which is only a napkin, but the *information* contained and revealed in the product.

Actually, the "information" is only "necessary" as a means-to-an-end. Face to gleaming face with the pirate's chest of jewels and doubloons, the napkin buyer may drop that napkin on the ground...

It's the *end* object, the *treasure* which animates the buyer's heart, and opens up his wallet freely.

In the same way, the *value* of learning how to work from home and make $1,000 per hour in a clean mail order business is a treasure! In spite of the simple Kinko's fact that – measured in terms of paper and ink – it only costs a couple bucks to print up. Printing's not the issue. The *treasure* is!

Believe me! You're learning all the secrets right now that make this kind of money available to you.

Same thing with a diet program. You're not selling a "manual" or a "video." You're selling a program that will make your client attractive to the opposite sex, and make her feel good about living again.

Successful marketers understand this distinction, and execute their programs with far greater success.

Always <u>sell</u> <u>the</u> <u>treasure</u>.

Same thing about an asset protection program. You're selling to a rich man who fears that the government, an attorney, an employee, or the public may try and take away what he's worked so hard to acquire. The value of preserving a multi-million dollar estate is not measured by how much it *costs* to manufacture a manual and a video tape.

The value of an information product is measured by the *benefit* it brings to the client's life.

It's not about how much 78 pages of a manual and 240 minutes of video tape cost... Just like romantic days of pirates and buried treasure, it's not the faded whisper of a napkin the client wants... *It's the treasure!*

Sell maps.

Easy And Cheap To Create And / Or Acquire

We've already seen how incredibly affordable information products are to "manufacture." No special equipment is required. You can do it all at your neighborhood copy shop.

But you've got to have something to copy, don't you? That's the most important thing, because if you don't have a product, you can't have a sale...

And not only the *product*, which is only ½ of the formula, but the *copy* too! A complete proven, working marketing plan. A sales letter that works!

There's 2 basic types of rights you can normally get to an information product. (I go into this whole subject more deeply, and discuss additional alternatives to acquiring a product in *How To Get Your Own Million Dollar Product*.)

You usually get either *resale* rights or *duplication* rights. Resale rights give you the opportunity to sell the product of another, using the effective copy that they've already tested and proven. You split the revenues. With duplication rights, also called *reprint* rights, *you* reproduce the product, ship it, bill for it, etc, and *you* keep <u>100% of the revenues</u>.

Incredibly, these rights can sometimes be *very easy* to acquire. You can frequently get high quality products to sell for *free!*

For example, in Diversified Resources we <u>give</u> every person who purchases *Paper Profit$* courses I, II, & III the resale rights to the courses.

The resale rights give the purchaser <u>2</u> *additional* ways to make money.

Number 1: Sell the courses. When you get the rights to a product AND marketing system that's completely setup, and <u>proven</u>, with a history of success – you've just taken the keys to the kingdom in your hands. No ads to write, no products to create, no special skills to operate it. <u>Guaranteed</u> to make money.

With the rights to the *Paper Profit$* Courses you have the opportunity to earn a *substantial* income. For instance, when someone purchases the $737.00 *Broker* course, you make $294.80 (40%). Three course sales alone, not counting the *notes* you broker, and you've made back all your money you invested in your course *PLUS* a profit!

And we do all the work, so all the profit is yours! We inventory the product, we ship the product, we run the credit card, we do the administrative work. You just market – where the real results come from – and deposit those big fat checks!

Our high man, Jim Mertz, a Kentuckian, liked cashing the $4,210.40 check he recently received. Keep that up for 12 months and you've got $50,524.80. He's got 12 deals on the board so far this month. Most of all he likes the independence that this kind of wealth gives him, because, you see, this is only one part of his income. Just check the mail occasionally, send the orders off to Diversified Resources for processing, and pocket the money. As regular as clockwork.

Number 2: Do more notes. The whole purpose of the *Paper Profit$* Course is to teach you how to broker "cash-flows" for a substantial profit – anywhere from $2,537 on the low end to upwards of $17,000 on the high end. (Actually, there is no upper limit. We've got one man working right now on a *single* deal with a $150,000 purse!) So...

The greatest thing is that, when you're selling courses, the people who buy from you will frequently bring their notes back to you. Want to hear about a home run? One of our affiliates snagged a client who's bringing him 8-12 notes a month. It's a rehabber in Minnesota. You figure that! If he's only earning $700 per note (discounted rate because of the number of notes he's doing), and only does 8, that's 8 x $700 = $5,600 per month. That's $67,200 per year for hardly lifting a finger!

You can get these opportunities for *free!*

Why Would We Do This For You?

Occasionally an incredulous person asks, "Why would you do this for me?"

You're an insider now. I want to tell you why. Think about it... By *sharing the wealth, we all have greater opportunities.* Myself included.

When you sell one of our courses, it's true, you get the lion's share of the profit. But, remember, there's still profit in it for me. Profit that I might not otherwise get. That's enough.

But, in the *backend*, there's *even more!* Most people take advantage of our *Paper Profit$ Hotline.* In fact, it's an indispensable weapon in the arsenal of success for beginning mortgage brokers. Well guess what? It's a *working line* – we *both* make money by doing deals. That's exciting!

Also, once these people enter into my database, I have the opportunity to make money off the backend – that is, from selling them <u>additional</u> <u>products</u>. Somewhere down the line. What if I'm putting on a seminar on brokering notes? Or a new software that makes the deals go faster? These people are ideal prospects, aren't they?

By the way, you'll notice that I keep approaching certain KEY IDEAS, like the *backend*, from many different angles. The purpose of this is to give you a well-rounded comprehension of the key wealth pivot points. These are the principles, concepts, and practices that have made fortunes. Ignorance of them – and this is the state that most business people labor under – destines you to a life of hard work and struggle...

By the way, we also have available duplication rights to a select number of *highly desirable* courses available to a limited number of marketers. If you're interested in this good-sense shortcut, you'd better contact us immediately. Don't sleep on it! Ask about "duplication rights."

The backend, including resale and reprint rights, is such an important topic that we offer a Special $197 Report that shows you how to set up a number of backend and *frontend* incomes! In it you'll find complete details, including actual working forms and agreements. I promise to tell you later how you can get this valuable report, "High Impact Backend Marketing," for *free!*

Easy To Handle

Handling information products is a breeze. I've got a close friend in the restaurant business... Throwing out food all the time... Food spoiling before he cooks it... Food spoiling after he cooks it...

It would take 3 years before something went bad on our shelves. But, as you'll see in the next section on "Publishing-On-Demand," we never have inventory sufficient to last 3 years... More like 3 days....

Shipping is easy with information products. No special boxes or packing required. Shipping damage is practically unheard of in the information industry. In the hundreds of thousands of products we've shipped out, we've <u>never</u> <u>had</u> <u>one</u> <u>returned</u> <u>defective</u>. Contrast this with the fact that it is shipping that kills a lot of more fragile products.

Plus, it's *cheap* to ship information products. Today there's a multitude of ways to ship these products, from the postal system, to UPS, to Airborne, to DHL, to a host of other easy options.

Info products are compact, and relatively lightweight. You couldn't find a better product to pack and ship, for low cost and no problems.

Easy To Produce: Publishing-On-Demand

One of the other multitudinous advantages this business offers is that you can do this whole business utilizing *publishing-on-demand*.

This makes it quick, incredibly easy, and even more outrageously profitable!

First of all, you've got to have a product to sell, right?

NO! You can sell it first, then, when you have all the money for it safely ensconced in your bank account, *then* make it!

The Entrepreneur's Dream. Literally, publishing-on-demand allows you to start your business on a shoestring!

Just trek on down to your neighborhood copy shop, give them your master, and wait while they run your manual.

We pay 2½¢ per page. You can too, if you explain that you'll be doing this regularly. But even if you have to pay 10¢ a page, the point is that you're paying with the customer's money – that you've already received! *Not yours!*

When you need to copy some cassettes, well, we buy our cassettes from Christian Duplicators (1-800-327-9332) for just 37¢ each. They also sell several high speed tape duplicators, so you can do your duplications in house, if you want to. We do. If you'd rather contract it out, you can find a "cassette duplicator" in your local yellow pages that will run them for $1.10 each, with labels. What could be easier?

You can copy videos on your home recorder or pay $2.00 - $3.50 each to a duplicator.

The three biggest killers of businesses are overhead, accounts receivable, and inventory. Operating your business by publishing-on-demand, you don't have to have any of these!

You don't have any overhead working from your home. None at all! No rent, no leases, no employees, no taxes, no nada.

You don't have any accounts receivables. Not in this business! What that's saying is that you don't have anyone owing you money. A debt they may be slow or negligent to pay. While expenses march on... You get your money up front!

And you don't have any inventory, a money eater for normal business, which has to pay for inventory before they sell it... Pay and pray to sell... I don't like it.

This publishing-on-demand feature of information marketing is much better! Don't you think?

Information Marketing – The Ultimate Business

Look no further! When you dream about direct response marketing of information products you've just discovered the world's *ultimate* business. One that showers oodles of money on you, while requiring very little of your work or effort. *THIS IS GOOD!*

So how do you get rich in information marketing? That *is* the question!

The answer is *get started!*

Ready, Fire! Aim...

It's the entrepreneur's creed. If you'll just get started with what you know at this point, you'll develop! There's a cybernetic feedback loop that refines and empowers your efforts. You learn to a point... then, *to actually make money, you must jump in* and play the game. Then, from the experience and insight of playing, combined with the knowledge you continue to mine from your courses, you apply your new learning to a higher level of performance. Continuously.

It's not complex. If you will do a *minimal amount* of passionately fun work. But most people won't, and they therefore never create a *life*... Thus, they remain roped and bound by their lousy j.o.b.

But this business offers you so much more than just money. It gives you a *lifestyle*! It gives you the total freedom and independence you want, need, and deserve – the *time* and the *money* to do what you want, when you want, where you want, with who you want.

Distinctly, *quality of life.*

2 *FREE Special BONUSES!*

FREE BONUS #1

Official Resale Rights License to *Mail and Grow Rich*

2 Versions of Sales Letter to *Mail and Grow Rich*

FREE BONUS #2

"Message to Friends Who Want To Become Millionaires"

by Ted Nicholas

®fficial Resale Rights License

*Document certifies that the non-exclusive product resale
and marketing copy reprint & duplication rights to*

MAIL AND GROW RICH

by **Ted Ciuba**

Have been transferred to you, the original purchaser/owner of this book –

(**$997** *Ca$h* **Value**)

Only 1 Condition

You must sell this book to everyone at the full price of $19.97

Simply collect $19.97 (+ 7.00 domestic shipping/handling,
$12 International) per book, then, forward 50% + shipping.
We'll ship the book(s) right out, directly to your customer!

This limited license also includes the right to use our
copyrighted *killer* proven sales letters (following). You'll
need to change the paragraphs that talk about ordering to fit
your particular situation. Put these letters on your word
processor, substitute your own contact information (name,
address, phone, fax, email, etc.). Extra Bonus! Since we're
always *optimizing* you can surf anytime up to
http://www.mailandgrowrich.com/mailrich and get the *latest
most POWERFUL* version of the sales letter existing! You can
also put it on the internet, and sell from your website. If you
want to link to us through an affiliate program and get paid for
the sales you send to our site, you can do it that way, too.
Check it out at http://www.mailandgrowrich.com. Of course,
you have to 1) leave the copyright notice – Copyright © 2000
by Ted Ciuba – in place, and 2) leave Ted Ciuba as the signer
to the sales letter. But when it comes time to send in the
money, *have them send it to you!*

You Can DO It!!!

For Parthenon Marketing, Inc,

[signature]

1 January 2000

Today's *Ultimate* Homebased Business!
A New Era of Opportunity in the 21st Century!

"Earn $3,288 In Less Than 1 Hour!"

© Ted Ciuba 2000

Technology Makes It Possible For Anyone To Run A Worldwide Business From Your Spare Bedroom!

Dear Friend,

Let's talk "mail order" – the way it's done today, in the 21st Century... Not the way it was done in the 1920's.

Excuse me. It's 9:06 a.m. and I've just been interrupted by the beautiful sound of the fax. I'm sitting at my desk in Nashville, Tennessee writing these very words you see. There's only 3 easy steps on level ground between my desk and my fax. A distributor is faxing in a $1,047 order.

It's so nice of him to do that for me. He lives in Midland, Texas, but his website spans the globe. A man from Ft. Lauderdale, Florida called him up. Then the distributor faxes me the credit card info and, *Voila!* that money's in *MY* bank account!

Mail Order Today

See what I'm talking about? The client saw the product on the *internet*, used the *phone* to order it, and our distributor uses the *fax* to transmit the order. I use my *computer*'s modem to run the credit card. I'll copy the manuals at *Insty-Print* and mail them out this afternoon. Nothing to it!

We set the website up for the distributor, by the way. Now he's churning in orders like this nearly every day.

Anyway... to continue! It's become *so easy!* Anyone who will dare to use today's simple technology can easily set up an automatic killer money-making machine!

But first, excuse me again. I've just been delightfully interrupted by the sound of the fax again! I just can't keep my composure when I hear that beautiful abbreviated *ring*. Next comes the *whirr-r-r* of a nice fat order. *Hmm.* This order has been passed on to me by one of our distributors in Connecticut. A lady on the opposite coast, in Inglewood, California wants to start with our Paper Profit$ I & II. A $247.90 order.

You Can Be Dumb Or Dumber And Still Succeed In This Business!

Once even the word "technology" impressed me. I was poor, too. Then I stumbled my way in. Easily... over the course of a few months I became rich and independent.

First I asked one of my friends to show me how, and 5 minutes later I could send and receive faxes. Then I went to the computer store and bought a computer. The friendly clerk advised me what I needed and showed me how to turn the computer on when I got home. A friend showed me in 30 minutes how to surf the worldwide web.

I put a *free* ad on America Online. It was then I first discovered the rocket power of cyber marketing! A few weeks later I quit my lousy job teaching at a prestigious university. That was several years ago. I got rich in the first few months. I think you can do the same thing. You see...

Please excuse me again. ... I've just been interrupted by my email software. It talks to me every time an order comes in. Another distributor sending in another $997 order. The customer completed the secure on-line order form on his site, *and here it is!* Total internet technology.

It's 10:05 a.m. As I was saying........

Oh, I'm sorry. Please excuse me one final time. After I take this telephone call I promise I'm going to get my laptop and go down to the first floor and write on the dining room table. Away from the profitable diversions of the phone and the fax.

But first... This is an affiliate on the line who we helped go independent. He enrolled in the full *Paper Profit$* program a few months ago. $737. Doing exactly what the manuals explained, Scott Pentecost earned a smacking $42,629.15 on his first deal. 'oday he wants me to take his credit card to the tune of $997.00. Not surprisingly, I might add.

Whew! That's better. Now that I'm downstairs I'll be able to finish this letter without thinking about all the money that I'm earning.

Oh, by the way. Fortunately, it's not important to have a whiz-bang web site that will purr-and-cat. The important thing is marketing. Check out my simple site at mailandgrowrich.com. Yet well over 60% of our business is web-related. You can do the same thing.

All you have to do is *get going!* The internet is so happening that today any moderately executed internet business can give you an independent living.

Review: I just made $3,288.90 in less than 1 hour. I didn't do a single bit of "work" to get this money! In fact, each order was a delightful interruption of the work I was trying to get done. Distributors, the information superhighway, and the fax did all the work for me. I chatted on the phone a little bit, with one customer. No high-pressure sales.

Everyone of these orders was web-related. My costs, once putting up my $100 per year web site, are totally zero. When you don't have to spend any big bucks to market, it *sure makes it easy!*

A Month's Take-Home Pay In An Hour

I'm a lot richer now than I was when I sat down an hour ago. My $3,288.90 for an hour's worth of hanging out is *greater than a month's take-home pay* for *millions* of "successful" Americans!

Well, that just about wraps up this session. I'm going back up to the 4th floor to "work" a little.

A Book Unlike Any Other

Fortunately for you, I've taken everything I've discovered and perfected in practice and simplified it down into a quick-reading book titled, *Mail and Grow Rich - How To Get Rich in "Mail Order" in the* Information Age*!*

In *Mail and Grow Rich* you get mail order laid bare, so that your very first venture can succeed beyond your wildest dreams! Just stick your eyeballs on these chapter titles! 1. Secrets To Earning $3,288 In Less Than 1 Hour, 2. Blowing The Lid Off The World's Most Profitable Business, 3. Information Marketing, 4. Reality Check 101, 5. "Mail Order" in the *Information Age!*" 6. The Principles of Wealth. Imagine what you'll learn!

Every one of these chapters takes you down in the trenches of this "mail order" opportunity, and shows you how you can make $100,000 from your kitchen table at home. You'll never be the same again.

I can't begin to describe the things you'll learn in this powerhouse 224 page book. For starters, you'll discover...

➤   How to start from home part-time with *zero* expenses
➤   In black and white just how easy it is to earn your 1st $1 million
➤   The most distinguishable secret of mail order, that virtually guarantees your success!
➤   The mechanics of the direct response business, and why it's the only business you should ever consider
➤   An internet strategy that can immediately take you to a $100,000 income, all by itself! Play it right, and the sky's the limit!

- ➤ Exactly why *Information Marketing* is so lucrative, with instant returns of *7,000%* and more...
- ➤ How to sell products you don't even own... with joint ventures
- ➤ Anyone with common sense, a desire to succeed, and a willingness to follow my step-by-step plan can succeed
- ➤ How to set this business up on complete auto-pilot!
- ➤ How to use distributors to turn the sale of a single product into an ongoing stream of income that earns you over $100,000!
- ➤ The truth about why your own credit absolutely doesn't matter at all. Learn about the secret sources that will process your credit cards, so you never lose an impulse sale!
- ➤ Why it's actually *easier* to sell more expensive – and more profitable! – products! Get your share!
- ➤ How to get millions of dollars worth of *free* advertising. Harold Moe spent a few ¢ents sending a press release to *Family Circle* and got $3,591,000 worth of orders in 60 days! That's more than most people earn in their entire lives!
- ➤ How to pyramid your profits to a multi-million dollar fortune!
- ➤ How to incorporate the Parthenon Strategy of Pre-Eminence so that you *both* make a quick killing AND last for a million dollar future. And there's *much, much* more!...

You can have all the wealth, security, freedom, and prestige that you crave. Literally, Financial Freedom is but months *or weeks* away!

It's Important Who You Learn From

Does my system work? Check out what others are saying!

I luv it when someone who has actually done something writes about how they have done it... telling you how you can do it, too. Ted Ciuba has done it. Mail and Grow Rich tells you how he did it and how you can do it. – Jim Straw, Cleveland, Tennessee

"It is so refreshing after many years of disappointments to finally come across an honest and honorable individual in the mail order industry. You not only offer exactly what you say you offer, but you should be selling your materials for ten times what you ask!" – Randall Mixon, Columbus, Georgia

"Being Christmas, we only took in $32,000 in December and $30,500 in January. Then we made another $46,000 in February and $88,000 in March.... I work less than 4 days a week, from home and have plenty of time to spend with my family." – Peter Sun, Australia

"The only course that has ever made me any money is yours! And I've spent bloody thousands on other courses!" $17,000 in 1 day. – Christian Naef, London, England

"I bought Ted's course in January of this year... I made an astonishing $18,895 within 5 weeks... Since that time I have done $1.985 million dollars worth of business. I now consider Ted Ciuba a valuable resource to my business and a close friend." – Greg Chaffin, Dallas, Texas

"It doesn't matter whether you're young or old, black or white, man or woman – these opportunities are available to everyone." – Los Angeles Times

Nobody Else Can Teach You This Stuff...

...because they don't know it. Sure, parroting the media, anybody can talk about the explosive growth of computers and the internet, but are they making good money every day from the telecommunications breakthroughs?

Mail and Grow Rich – *100% Guaranteed*

You might find it hard to believe, but *Mail and Grow Rich* is only $19.97.

And it's 100% guaranteed. You, and you alone decide if "Mail Order" in the *Information Age* will work for you. You may return the book anytime within 30 days for a prompt, cheerful no-questions-asked refund. How could I be more fair?

Free Bonus When You Send For Your Copy Today

In fact, I'll give you 2 valuable bonuses! FREE BONUS #1! I'll *give* you a license to resale *Mail and Grow Rich*, and keep a full 50% of the revenues! This could be your first product in a prosperous new future! Plus I'll give you 2 different *killer* sales letters to sell it like crazy! Value $997.

FREE BONUS #2! You couldn't pay Ted Nicholas any amount of money to give you his undivided 'attention. A self-made millionaire 100x over, he's also the highest paid writer in the world. Yet he poured his heart and soul into "Message To Friends Who Want To Become Millionaires." Value $177. You get *both* these bonuses *FREE!*

But I Do Have 1 Condition

The philosophies, principles, strategies, and techniques you learn in *Mail and Grow Rich* are absolutely awesome. You learn to strategically unleash a whole network of powerful psychological principles of human persuasion. The power it gives you over other human beings is staggering!

That's my point... If you don't think you can be entirely honest and work for the well-being of humanity, then I absolutely refuse to sell to you.

How To Get Started Today

To order with your MasterCard, Visa, American Express, Novus/Discover, or *check-by-phone* call toll-free 24-hours a day 1-877-4 *RICHES*.

Or fill out the No Risk Rush Request with your payment info and get it to us whatever way you like. Fax: +615-662-3108. Mail: Parthenon Marketing, Inc; 2400 Crestmoor Rd #36; Nashville TN 37215

This book has been printed in the US under a special license arrangement with an independent publisher and this offer is a limited price test. The price will soon be substantially higher. Also I can't guarantee how long I'll keep the *Resale License* as a bonus. Don't hate yourself for missing out on this no risk offer act today!

Mail and Grow Rich!

Ted Ciuba

Ted Ciuba, Marketer, Marketing Consultant

P.S. To make it doubly good for you, I stopped the presses at the last minute to add <u>another</u> <u>bonus</u>! You'll learn exactly... "How To Unleash Your Own Million Dollar Potential."

P.P.S. Have you whipped the pencil to it? Today, literally as I sat down to write this letter, the fax rang... Less than an hour later I was $3,288.90 richer. What if I only <u>work 1 hour a week</u>, and then, since I enjoy such independence, take off the entire months of July and December? Try this: 44 weeks x 1 hour x $3,288.90/hour = $144,711.60 per year!

To get your share, order your copy and *Mail and Grow Rich* today!

No Risk Rush Request for *Mail and Grow Rich*　　Offer 101

✔ Yes, Ted, please rush me ___ copies of your book, *Mail and Grow Rich*, at $19.97 per copy (+$7 s/h, $12 International) on the understanding that if I'm not delighted I can return it within 30 days for a prompt refund.

> Your Name
> Your Contact Info

Call, mail, fax, or email this form or this information!

Name:_____

Address:_____

City/St/Zip_____

Phone/fax_____

Email:_____

Card# _____

Signature_____

___ Cash, check, or money order enclosed

___ Charge my card: [ ] Visa [ ] MasterCard
　　　　　　　　[ ] AMEX [ ] Novus/Discover

Exp date_____

Date_____

Attention Anyone Who Wants To Work At Home In A Clean Respectable Business
The Genuine Opportunity To Live Your Dreams!

How I Earned $3,115 Last Weekend
By Not Doing Anything –
And How You Can Do The Same Thing
© Ted Ciuba 2000

Dear Friend,

Money. I'm writing this letter about <u>you</u> and <u>money</u>.

I put together a little parttime business venture. You see, I really like to spend my time in love with my family. So I only allow myself a few hours "work" each day - if you can call doing what you passionately love to do *working* - yet that business frequently earns me more than $3,000 per day.

Make Money When You Work, Make Money When You Don't

Last week I took Thursday, Friday, and Saturday and went and flew out to see my good friend Brian Keith Voiles up in Salt Lake City. 100% tax deductible, even though I had a *great time!* We talked about advertising. Now, listen close, Friend. I wasn't even in the office, I wasn't even in town, I never once answered my phone! Yet when I went to check the fax in my spare bedroom, I was overwhelmed! I had $3,115.50 worth of sales!

Don't get me wrong... $3,115.50 is not solely the impressive thing... We mark our success in $3,000 days.... and $3,000 hours. And this was a long weekend. But what is impressive is that these days I wasn't even tending the ship! <u>This all came in with no active effort on my part</u>!

$636 Per Hour

And yesterday, God bless him, I took the afternoon off to be with my teenage son. School let out early, so we went shopping for new tennis shoes. Then enjoyed pizza together at the Alien Eatery. *This* is what life's about! I didn't "ask" or explain to anybody, I just went.

It's against my religion to work before 10am. If you call and get me earlier than that, *it's a miracle!* But, I did work about 2 hours before I went. It was a fast-paced 2 hours while I raked in $1,496. I returned to my home office around 4:30 and gladly took another $413.50 from a customer who made me work past 5:00! He wanted overnight shipping, so I carried his package to Mail Boxes Etc, right away. Do the math! That's $1,909.50 worth of business in 3 hours. Hmmm... How would you like to work 3 hours at $636.33 PER HOUR!

And today, as I write this letter, on a Tuesday, working about 4 hours, I've already pulled in $8,272.60. That's $2,068.15 per hour.

On one of my favoritest days I earned $15,465.97. Not only for the money, but because it was on my wife's birthday. Need I say it's a great life?!!!

What Is This Amazing Business?

It's one that's been around for years, but it's never been so easy for the ordinary guy to get into it and to make a lot of money.

It's *mailorder*. Only it's actually grown past strictly "mail" order. In fact, it's more accurate to call it *direct response marketing*. These techniques are easy, precise, predictable, cheap to implement, and powerfully profitable! I call it "Mail Order" in the *Information Age*.

You see, *today* there's little things we take for granted - like the phone, a fax, your computer, and the neighborhood copy machine - that make it possible for you to do from your desktop what it used to take a major corporation to do. You can literally <u>run</u> <u>a</u> <u>worldwide</u> <u>business</u> <u>from</u> <u>a</u> <u>corner</u> <u>of</u> <u>your</u> <u>room</u>!

When you learn the success secrets of *modern* mailorder, you find that the amount of money you make is *NOT* connected to the time or effort you put in.

These secrets work for *any* product or service. You just have to learn how to cash in on this boom for yourself.. That's because when you apply your skills in the biggest market in history, today's booming *Information Age*, you can quickly, easily, safely, and insanely enjoy all the time, money, and freedom you want to do whatever you want in life!

A Book Unlike Any Other

Fortunately for you, I've taken everything I've discovered and perfected in practice and simplified it down into a quick-reading book titled, *Mail and Grow Rich - How To Get Rich in "Mail Order" in the* Information Age*!*

In *Mail and Grow Rich* you get mail order laid bare, so that your very first venture can succeed beyond your wildest dreams! Just stick your eyeballs on these chapter titles! 1. Secrets To Earning $3,288 In Less Than 1 Hour, 2. Blowing The Lid Off The World's Most Profitable Business, 3. Information Marketing, 4. Reality Check 101, 5. "Mail Order" in the *Information Age!*" 6. The Principles of Wealth. Imagine what you'll learn!

Every one of these chapters takes you down in the trenches of this "mail order" opportunity, and shows you how you can make $100,000 from your kitchen table at home. You'll never be the same again.

I can't begin to describe the things you'll learn in this powerhouse 224 page book. For starters, you'll discover...

➤ How to start from home part-time with *zero* expenses

➤ In black and white just how easy it is to earn your first $1 million

➤ The most distinguishable secret of mail order, that virtually guarantees your success!

➤ The mechanics of the direct response business, and why it's the only business you should ever consider

➤ An internet strategy that can immediately take you to a $100,000 income, all by itself! Play it right, and the sky's the limit!

➤ Exactly why *Information Marketing* is so lucrative, with instant returns of *7,000%* and more...

➤ How to sell products you don't even own... with joint venture partners.

➤ How anyone with common sense, a desire to succeed, and a willingness to follow my step-by-step plan can succeed

➤ How to set this business up on complete auto-pilot!

➤ How to use distributors to turn the sale of a single product into an ongoing stream of income that earns you over $100,000!

➤ The truth about why your own credit absolutely doesn't matter at all. Learn about the secret sources that will process your credit cards, so you never lose an impulse sale!

➤ Why it's actually *easier* to sell expensive - more profitable! - products!

➤ How to get millions of dollars worth of *free* advertising. Harold Moe spent a few ¢ents sending a press release to *Family Circle* and got $3,591,000 worth of orders in 60 days! That's more than most people earn in their entire lives!

➤ How to pyramid your profits into a multi-million dollar fortune!

➤ How to incorporate the Parthenon Strategy of Pre-Eminence so that you *both* make a quick killing AND last for a million dollar future. And there's *much, much* more!...

You can have all the wealth, security, freedom, and prestige that you crave. Literally, Financial Freedom is but months *or weeks* away!

It's Important Who You Learn From

Does my system work? Check out what other~ are saying!

I luv it when someone who has actually done something writes about how they have done it... telling you how you can do it, too. Ted Ciuba has done it. Mail and Grow Rich tells you how he did it and how you can do it. - Jim Straw, Cleveland, Tennessee

"It is so refreshing after many years of disappointments to finally come across an honest and honorable individual in the mail order industry. You not only offer exactly what you say you offer, but you should be selling your materials for ten times what you ask!" - Randall Mixon, Columbus, Georgia

"Being Christmas, we only took in $32,000 in December and $30,500 in January. Then we made another $46,000 in February and $88,000 in March.... I work less than 4 days a week, from home and have plenty of time to spend with my family." - Peter Sun, Australia

"The only course that has ever made me any money is yours! And I've spent bloody thousands on other courses!" $17,000 in 1 day. - Christian Naef, London, England

"I bought Ted's course in January of this year... I made an astonishing $18,895 within 5 weeks... Since that time I have done $1.985 million dollars worth of business. I now consider Ted Ciuba a valuable resource to my business and a close friend." - Greg Chaffin, Dallas, Texas

I made my first sale for $535.90 the 2nd day I owned Ted's course. - Scott Sossamon, Duncan, Oklahoma

"It doesn't matter whether you're young or old, black or white, man or woman - these opportunities are available to everyone." - Los Angeles Times

Nobody Else Can Teach You This Stuff...

...because they don't know it. Sure, parroting the media, anybody can talk about the explosive growth of computers and the internet, but are they making good money every day from the telecommunications breakthroughs?

Mail and Grow Rich - *100% Guaranteed*

You might find it hard to believe, but *Mail and Grow Rich* is only $19.97.

And it's 100% guaranteed. You, and you alone decide if "Mail Order" in the *Information Age* will work for you. You may return the book anytime within 30 days for a prompt, cheerful no-questions-asked refund. How could I be fairer?

Free Bonus When You Send For Your Copy Today

In fact, I'll give you 2 valuable bonuses! FREE BONUS #1! I'll give you a license to resale *Mail and Grow Rich*, and keep a full 50% of the revenues! This could be your first product in a prosperous new future! Plus I'll give you 2 different *killer* sales letters to sell it like crazy! Value $997.

FREE BONUS #2! You couldn't pay Ted Nicholas any amount of money to give you his undivided attention. A self-made millionaire 100x over, he's also the highest paid writer in the world. Yet he poured his heart and soul into "Message To Friends Who Want To Become Millionaires." Value $177. You get *both* these bonuses *FREE!*

But I Do Have 1 Condition

The philosophies, principles, strategies, and techniques you learn in *Mail and Grow Rich* are absolutely awesome. You learn to strategically unleash a whole network of powerful psychological principles of human persuasion. The power it gives you over other human beings is staggering!

That's my point... If you don't think you can be entirely honest and work for the well-being of humanity, then I absolutely refuse to sell to you.

How To Get Started Today

To order with your MasterCard, Visa, American Express, Novus/Discover, or *check-by-phone* call toll-free 24-hours a day 1-877-*4 RICHES*.

Or fill out the No Risk Rush Request with your payment info and get it to us whatever way you like. Fax: +615-662-3108. Mail: Parthenon Marketing, Inc; 2400 Crestmoor Rd #36; Nashville TN 37215 USA. You can also send your information via email to ordermr@mailandgrowrich.com

This book has been printed in the US under a special license arrangement with an independent publisher and this offer is a limited price test. The price will soon be substantially higher. Also I can't guarantee how long I'll keep the *Resale License* as a bonus. Don't hate yourself for missing out on this no risk offer act today!

Mail and Grow Rich!

Ted Ciuba, Marketer, Marketing Consultant

P.S. To make it doubly good for you, I stopped the presses at the last minute to add another bonus! You'll learn exactly... "How To Unleash Your Own Million Dollar Potential."

P.P.S. I know what I'm saying may be hard to believe. Your family members, your friends, teachers, preachers, and political figures are telling you, "If it sounds to good to be true - it is." Yet, are they millionaires? Or are they instead living lives of economic desperation like the mass of humanity? Whose advice do you think you should take?

No Risk Rush Request for *Mail and Grow Rich*   Offer 101

✔ Yes, Ted, please rush me ___ copies of your book, *Mail and Grow Rich*, at $19.97 per copy (+$7 s/h, $12 International) on the understanding that if I'm not delighted I can return it within 30 days for a prompt refund.

> Your Name
> Your Contact Info

Call, mail, fax, or email this form or this information!

Name:_____
Address:_____
City/St/Zip_____
Phone/fax_____
Email:_____
Card#_____
Signature_____

___ Cash, check, or money order enclosed
___ Charge my card: [ ] Visa [ ] MasterCard
[ ] AMEX [ ] Novus/Discover

Exp date_____
Date_____

To place your orders, photocopy this page, (or rip it out if you have to), or include this information on your own paper...

RESELLER MAIL AND GROW RICH Order Form

Your Name:_____

Address1:_____

Address2:_____

   Phone:_____Email:_____

_____

Customer Name:_____

Address1:_____

Address2:_____

   Phone:_____Email:_____

Customer Name:_____

Address1:_____

Address2:_____

   Phone:_____Email:_____

Please ship immediately. I have included cash, check, money order, or my own credit card number in the amount of **$16.97** (50% of $19.97 = $9.97 + $7 s/h) **for every book** sold for U.S. delivery, $21.97 ($9.97 + $12 s/h) for International delivery.

# of Books	X	Amount incl. shipping	Equals	Extended Value
	X	$16.97 U.S. $21.97 International	Equals	$

Card #_____ Expiry_____

Signed_____ Date_____

NOTE: Checks are cleared electronically for *immediate shipping.*

Parthenon Marketing, Inc * 2400 Crestmoor Rd #36 * Nashville TN 37215 * +615-662-3169 / fax: +615-662-3108

Rush to:

ordermr@mailandgrowrich.com
+615-662-3169 / fax: +615-662-3108

Parthenon Marketing, Inc
2400 Crestmoor Rd #36
Nashville TN 37215

To place your orders, simply photocopy this page, (or rip it out if you have to), or include this information on your own paper...

RESELLER **MAIL AND GROW RICH** Order Form

Your Name:_____

Address1:_____

Address2:_____

    Phone:_____Email:_____

_____

Customer Name:_____

Address1:_____

Address2:_____

    Phone:_____Email:_____

Customer Name:_____

Address1:_____

Address2:_____

    Phone:_____Email:_____

Please ship immediately. I have included cash, check, money order, or my own credit card number in the amount of **$16.97** (50% of $19.97 = $9.97 + $7 s/h) **for every book** sold for U.S. delivery, $21.97 ($9.97 + $12 s/h) for International delivery.

# of Books	X	Amount incl. shipping	Equals	Extended Value
	X	$16.97 U.S. $21.97 International	Equals	$

Card #_____ Expiry_____

Signed_____ Date_____

NOTE: Checks are cleared electronically for *immediate shipping.*

Parthenon Marketing, Inc * 2400 Crestmoor Rd #36 * Nashville TN 37215 * +615-662-3169 / fax: +615-662-3108

Rush to:

ordermr@mailandgrowrich.com
+615-662-3169 / fax: +615-662-3108

Parthenon Marketing, Inc
2400 Crestmoor Rd #36
Nashville TN 37215

For Readers of *Mail and Grow Rich*!

Personal letter of advice from Ted Nicholas, author of million seller "How To Form Your Own Corporation Without A Lawyer For Under $75." (1,000,000 copies @ $19.97 = $19,970,000!)

A living legend in direct mail. Starting with a $90 ad, he went from his living room to a $200 *Million* direct response Fortune!

Article originally published in Ted Nicholas' "Direct Marketing Success Letter," February 23, 1995.

"Message to Friends Who Want To Become Millionaires"

Dear Friend:

This issue of DMSL is a real change of pace. It's dedicated to your friends and loved ones.

As your success grows, many people will ask for your assistance on their business endeavors. I'm sure you will do all you can to help. So to give you food for thought, I've devoted this issue of DMSL advising would-be millionaires!

People often approach me to help mentor their business success. For example, recently John, a friend, called. John is a mid-level manager in a large company. The conversation went something like this:

John: "I'm getting bored with my job. Direct marketing looks like a great way to build wealth. I'm interested in getting rich. I would like to learn all I can from you. Perhaps be a protégé. I know a lot of what you teach is in your books, tapes, and live seminars. However, at the moment I

don't have any money to invest in these materials
and programs."

My reaction usually is to seek more information.
After John granted me permission to ask some
personal questions, here is how the conversation
proceeded.

Ted: "I notice you're driving a new 1995
automobile. Do you mind telling me what your
payments are?" **John:** "$395 a month."

Ted: "Approximately what did you spend on your
week's vacation this past year?" **John:** $1800."

Ted: "You live in a new apartment building. What
is your current monthly rent?" **John:** "$750 a
month."

Undoubtedly you see where my questions lead. I
wanted to get a sense of John's values. The
foregoing answers already communicate volumes about
John.

I think it's safe to say he will <u>never</u> become a
millionaire. Not as long as he continues to think
the way he does. And most Americans unfortunately
share the same values.

The big problem? A profound lack of understanding
of what it takes to succeed. The most important
element in anyone's potential business success
is...

Education!

The price of business success is very simple. A
good education.

I feel that education in the U.S. is greatly
under-valued by nearly everyone. Except by super
successful entrepreneurs!

This may sound self-serving. But there is no other
way of communicating the reality. As a marketer of
"how to" information, a source of constant
fascination to me is that my very <u>best customers</u>
are also the <u>most successful</u>. Subscribers of Direct

Marketing Success Letter and buyers of my videos, audio tapes, and books, I'm proud to say, are among the best-known marketers in the world. And the richest!

The underlying reason for their outstanding success?

They <u>value education</u> so much they seek and pay for it.

They know knowledge about their career is an asset more priceless than gold. And, unlike money, jewels, real estate, stocks, all of which can be lost or taken away, what you know is yours forever.

Education can <u>never</u> be taken away. The super successful seem to instinctively know this. So they've become perpetual students. Always interested in learning something new. Constantly reading. And listening to tapes. Seeking out seminars conducted by doers who "walk the talk."

Those who are unsuccessful have bought into ideas that are not advancing their wealth production. Instead of investing in their own knowledge, they prefer to spend their money on cars, boats, planes, apartments, vacations, gadgets, etc.

The unsuccessful are unaware of this reality. It's impossible to succeed big in any field without a lot of knowledge.

There are just two ways to get the reality tested information you need which works in the real world:

1. The school of hard knocks - trial and error method

2. Books, tapes, seminars offered by those who have proven themselves.

Back to John. He tells me he really wants to hear my honest views. It's been said that "when the student is ready the teacher appears." I believe John. Here, then, is the advice I gave my friend.

Ted: "I'm going to give you ideas and suggestions. If you follow them your future success is guaranteed.

However, there is a catch. Your comfort level may be affected. Many ideas won't feel right at first. The recommendations are unconventional. Chances are you've never in your life received advice like I'm about to give you – from anyone. So some of it might sound strange and make you uncomfortable. That's OK. It is to be expected. As we learn and grow, our belief systems must be re-examined. And if necessary, changed.

1. The first thing you need to do on your path to success is completely **stop acting** on the **advice of friends, relatives**, and **teachers**. However well-meaning they are, their advice will **not** be helpful. Unless they are self-made millionaires. One must have lived and experienced being an entrepreneur. Otherwise no one can understand what is required.

    Indeed, you may have to find new friends. Negative ones can really hold you back. If you have a supportive mate or spouse, terrific. If you don't, a tough decision will have to be made. There may be no choice but to leave the relationship.

    You **must** have support. Negative people are influential. More than you realize. Don't just walk away from them. Run!

2. Begin immediately to **get out of debt**. Since your car payments are too big in relation to your income, **sell your car at once**. If you can do without a car and walk for awhile, great.

    My father taught me a great lesson. Automobiles are the biggest financial liability anyone can have. No investment you will ever make loses its value so quickly.

    If you feel you need a car, get a used one. Pay cash for it. Fortunately, the U.S. is one of the few countries in the world where you can get a good used car cheap.

3. **Move to a one-bedroom apartment**, or **look for a roommate or two** to share your apartment costs. Since you are single and have a two-bedroom apartment, you can easily slash your rent by half or more.

4. **Vacation creatively**. Instead of going to an expensive resort for a week, this year go to 2 or more good seminars that will advance your knowledge.

I'm sure you can do more to slash overhead. You could reduce or eliminate the big cost of interest your debts are causing. But, just by the suggested steps you will immediately have over $900 per month! Every saved cent can and should go toward your direct marketing education! It will be the best investment you have or will ever make.

You can begin investing in your long-neglected but potentially most valuable asset -

Yourself

5. **Start a success library** of your own. At minimum buy these books. Study and read them as soon as you can.

Confessions Of An Advertising Man by David Ogilvy
The Robert Collier Letter Book by Robert Collier
My Life in Advertising/Scientific Advertising by Claude Hopkins
How To Make Your Advertising Make Money by John Caples
Making Ads Pay by John Caples
The First Hundred Million by E. Haldeman-Julius
How To Make More Money With Your Direct Mail by Edward N. Mayer
The Mirror Makers by Stephen Fox
The Greatest Direct Mail Sales Letter Of All Times by Richard S. Hodgson
The 100 Greatest Advertisements by Julian Lewis Watkins
Million Dollar Mailings by Dennison Hatch
Atlas Shrugged by Ayn Rand
The Fountainhead by Ayn Rand

How I Found Freedom in an Unfree World by Harry
Browne
Ageless Body / Timeless Mind by Deepak Chopra
The Mysterious Cause and Cure of Illness by Dr.
John Matsen

Plus, get the following products as soon as
possible:

- *The Golden Mailbox - How to Get Rich in
  Direct Marketing* by Ted Nicholas
- *How I Sold $200 Million Worth of Products
  and Services* by Ted Nicholas
- *Direct Marketing Success Letter* - all back
  issues
- *Ted Nicholas Self Publishing Seminar Tapes*
- *Ted Nicholas Direct Marketing Seminar
  Videos*

6. **Join the following organizations**:

   Toastmasters. Regardless of what field you
   choose, when you learn to speak clearly and
   confidently it will help you.
   Direct Marketing Association, New York. Get
   their mailings and go to some of their
   seminars.
   Local Direct Marketing Association if you have
   one in your area.

7. **Get on good mailing lists**. Well-run direct
   marketing companies' mailings are important.
   Getting on their mailing lists is part of your
   education. Ask to be put on the following
   companies' lists, or buy something from them.

   Phillips Publishing
   Agora Publishing
   Nightingale Conant
   DELL Computer
   Reader's Digest
   The Company Corporation, Wilmington,
   Delaware
   Fischer Publishing, Canfield, Ohio
   Nicholas Direct, Inc., Indian Rocks Beach,
   Florida

8. **<u>Subscribe to these magazines</u>**:

<u>Direct Marketing</u>
<u>Direct</u>
<u>Direct Mail News</u>
<u>Economist</u>
<u>Entrepreneur</u>

9. **<u>Subscribe to these newsletters</u>**:

<u>Health and Healing</u>, Phillips Publishing
<u>Forecasts and Strategies</u>, Phillips
Publishing
<u>Who's Mailing What</u>, Target Marketing
<u>Direct Marketing Success Letter</u>

10. **<u>Seminars to attend</u>**:

DMA Seminars
Dan Kennedy Seminars
Jeff Paul Seminars
Gary Halbert Seminars
Peter Lowe Seminars
Dan Peña Seminars
Ted Nicholas Seminars

TIP: *When money is really tight, offer to work at seminars which interest you in return for free attendance. Many promoters will happily hire you to help sell tapes, etc.*

A note of caution. Be wary of whose advice you choose to follow at seminars or on tape. Most college professors and ad agency people are not teaching reality. They teach theory, which often sounds good, but does not work in the real world. Entrepreneur speakers who invest their own money in their own companies and who teach what they do every day are special. What they offer you is <u>invaluable</u>.

11. **<u>Learn to write sales copy</u>**. The most financially lucrative skill you can possess is the ability to write effective sales copy. There are two ways to learn.

   A. <u>Get a part-time job in commission sales</u>. New York Life or CIGNA Insurance, Amway,

Mary Kay, Fuller Brush, Encyclopedia Britannica, Kirby Vacuums, can all be excellent training ground for direct marketing. But, here is the key. Find an organization with a good sales manager to train you. Capable trainers often exist within leading direct sales organizations.

B. <u>Practice</u>. (After you read the previously mentioned books.) You don't have to be a great creative writer. But, you do need to develop sales skills. Good copy is "salesmanship in print." An excellent way to develop skill is to take a piece of successful copy that is working, such as an ad or sales letter. Write it out in long hand. It's great practice. You'll also begin to get a good feel for the writer's thinking process.

12. **Get a part-time job in a mail order company**. Here is an approach you can use that almost never fails. Find out who the direct marketing companies are in your area. Choose one or two with whom you'd like to work. Approach them. Explain how you can help them. Make this nearly impossible to resist offer. Include in your proposal this statement. You will help the employer make or save money. Or you'd rather quit or be let go anyway. And mean it. Offer to work <u>free</u> for at least two weeks! You will have a lot of takers. There would be absolutely no risk on the employer's part.

After you are hired, learn all you can about what it takes to operate the business.

13. **Start your own mail order business in your spare time**. What to sell? Choose a product or service that is now under-marketed. Acquire the rights to the product (see DMSL August, 1993). I recommend you begin by offering a free special report. Choose a hot subject you know, can learn, or acquire

the rights to. You then can sell a product to those who request your special report.

14. **Take a low-level job with a worthwhile company**. Many college graduates and MBAs can't get a job today. One of the big reasons is their unwillingness to take a lower level job which they consider "beneath" them.

That's precisely one of the reasons which underlies why minorities make up the biggest portion of the new millionaires in the U.S. They are willing to take any job, no matter how humble. Just for the chance to work and earn money!

There are many such examples. Sam Yeoung, a 23-year-old man originally from China took an entry level job at McDonald's 1½ years ago. His pay? Minimum wage. Within 6 months he was the assistant manager of the restaurant. Then he became manager. Today he is a district manager earning a six-figure income. Next year he will open his own McDonald's. My guess is he'll be a millionaire in less than 5 years.

Do you think a typical American-born college graduate would take such a position? No way! Instead, they might spend months, even years, collecting unemployment. The new millionaires create their own career. The real opportunity makers have learned how to capitalize on the smallest chance.

There are no bad jobs! Take any job. And do it extremely well, as best you can. Result? You'll create the ultimate job security. How? You'll make yourself indispensable to the business.

15. **Join the U.S. Marines**! Recently a survey showed that 66% of the CEOs of Fortune 500 companies were former Marines. (Of course

I'm not biased, but I also happen to be a former Marine.)

Do you think there is any relationship between CEOs rising to the top of their organizations and the world-famous discipline learned in the "Corps"? Of course there is!

Besides, John, I've never met anyone who couldn't use some more discipline. Have you?

16. **Do whatever is necessary to succeed**. When the going get tough, as it inevitably will at times, stop whimpering, "I'm doing the best I can." This is not good enough for a truly successful life. And it isn't worthy of you.

There is only one thing good enough.

You must do what is necessary.

When the banks turned Dan Peña down nearly 200 times, he kept contacting the next one. He got the financing. Today he is worth $200 million. Would you have given up at 6? Or 12? Or 50?

Colonel Sanders began at age 66 with assets of a broken down jalopy and a chicken recipe. He went to nearly 2,000 restaurants and was turned down. He kept going. When he was asked what he would have done if the 2,001st turned him down, he said, "I would have gone on to the 2,002nd!" Most people would have quit long before this. When would you have stopped?

I started my first business with savings of $800 and debts of $96,000. Numerous people turned me down. My bank also rejected my proposal. They told me I was crazy, the idea would never work. But I would not be denied. I knew I would find willing backers. And I did.

Most of the reason for my success today as a marketer, copywriter and entrepreneur is not more talent than others. What is the reason? I dig deeper than most people. I write 200 or more headlines for every product to find the right one. Others write 2 or 3 and expect a miracle. I study products strictly from the buyer's point of view. I write more copy drafts. I'm willing to try more tests and to fail more often than others. But here's the secret. I succeed more often, too!

The real secret is to:

Work harder at doing whatever is necessary!

"You, John, must do whatever is necessary to succeed. You will become a millionaire or whatever else you want to become! It's just inevitable."

As you read these words, you may be feeling that the path to direct marketing success is steeper than you first realized. And that sacrifices have to be made.

Here is the reality. There is a price to pay for success. And a price to pay for lack of achievement. You, like all of us, have a choice. To succeed in a big way, gratification may have to be delayed.

But the good news is, it's worth it! I believe there is no wasted energy in the universe. During those tough times when things look bleak, which happens in all our lives, I give myself a reminder for just as night follows day the results will come.

Yes, once you pay the price for success, the rewards will come. And keep coming forever! You will become as wealthy as you desire.

People all over the world will seek you out to buy your products. Invite you to speak. Offer you large sums to help them - be their partner. Present you with more opportunities than you could ever pursue.

And life is long. Gratification won't be delayed
forever. There is plenty of time to own fancy cars,
enjoy luxurious vacations, mansions, jewelry,
whatever you want. You'll be able to live the
lifestyle you choose anywhere in the world.

So dear reader, the above is what I offer my
friends. And yours. I look forward to getting your
feedback to this issue of DMSL. Looking forward to
next month.

Sincerely,

Ted Nicholas

P.S.   Next month in response to subscriber
        requests I will cover: How to Successfully
        Market Through Catalogues.

## Chapter 4

Reality Check 101

————— •••••••• —————

You're about to get rich. Really rich. But things are not so fair for most of your brethren. They work too hard, never having enough time for themselves and their families. Churches, little league and Girl Scouts, clubs, and maybe some effort at self-improvement, and they're all worn out.

Even with all negative stresses of distinctly *unquality* time at work, they don't have nearly enough money.

How did things get so turned around? Somehow, they manage to keep living month to mouth. Budgeting purchases of less than $200! Life has got them roped so tightly sometimes they think that *is* life! And so they turn on the TV again, and settle into numb and dumber.

But, do you want a little reality shock? Have you ever heard of Pareto? I'll bet you have...

The Pareto Principle

What you're about to learn here may sound basic. That's okay – *it is!* It's *so* basic, in fact, that it's the <u>foundation</u> of your success.

Pareto was an Italian mathematician who was the first to notice an interesting natural phenomenon. In the tradition of the times, tagging his discovery with his own name, he christened this 80/20 phenomenon the "Pareto Principle."

These 20% and 80% ratios make for some brutal realities in life. There's an inverse proportion set up, an imbalance that always exaggerates both the work and the rewards... To your gain or to your pain.

One way of explaining the principle is to say that 20% of the effort accomplishes 80% of the work.

This phenomenon holds true in just about any application. Personally, 20% of your friends give you 80% of your satisfaction. As a student, 80% of the time you spend studying only gives you 20% of your grade; you get 80% of your grade from 20% of your effort.

It's well known in the sales profession that 20% of the sales force produces 80% of the results.

Reality Chicklet: **Work less, earn more!**

When it comes to money, it's the smaller 20% of the population, 20 people out of 100, which gets the massive 80% rewards. That means that 80% of the people are fighting at the trough for the 20% left-overs.

As a humanitarian, I wish I could contravene this phenomenon, but it would be like trying to deny or ignore any other natural process, such as those that make the winds howl when winter comes. It doesn't do any good to be in denial.

However, remember that, *though we can't make the winds stop blowing, we can use them to our commercial purposes.* We can use the winds to sail our good-laden ships across oceans and with picturesque and pleasing windmills grind our grain into flour.

The simple truth is, *you don't have to be on the wrong side!!!* The whole purpose of this book is to give you the information, resources, and motivation you need to explode through the quantum barrier and forever enjoy the rewards of the magic 20%, the Upper Fifth.

...Doing a mere 20% of the work of those who suffer.
...Enjoying an exponential amount *more* money.

In special honor to Seignior Pareto, let's do the math. Then, in special honor of you, let's discuss the revolutionary truths dis-covered in his simple sounding principle.

Thought Experiment: The Pareto Principle and Money:

Let's apply this principle to a $2,000,000 pool of annual income, earned by 10 people.

Driving on Upper Fifth, Walking on Lower Broad

Preliminary Calculations	*Upper Fifth*	*Lower Broad*
Total persons	10	10
Applied %	20%	80%
Persons to split among	2	8
Total annual earnings	$2,000,000.00	$2,000,000.00
Applied %	80%	20%
Total money to divide	$1,600,000.00	$400,000.00
Applied Calculations		
Group money to divide	$1,600,000.00	$400,000.00
Divide by # of persons	2	8
Money per *person*	**$800,000.00**	**$50,000.00**

If you're in a normal crowd, those on Lower Broad, that can seem bad! The **"average" family** has to scrape by on **$50,000 per year**.

That would be hard enough, but you have to meanwhile see each of the few well-to-do families on Upper Fifth enjoying the best of life with **$800,000 *each*!**

There are people who exclaim, *"That's no fair!"*

Successful direct marketers don't have much to do with this crowd... Except for the few of us who actually make efforts to raise their consciousness, *so that they can become rich too.*

$800,000 per person for the achiever
- versus -
$50,000 per year for the "average" Joe

Reality Check. It's available to you – *if you WANT it!* There are secrets, but they're available to anyone who searches.

The truth is,

> Wealth is not *given* to you, but
> neither is it *withheld* from you.

But look, these figures reveal even more dramatic results!

Revealing! The *Real* Average In Any "Average"!

FACT: Get out your pencil and prove it to yourself! Each of the 8 out of 10 average persons receives, as his or her individual share, a mere 2.5% of the available money and resources.

According to the mean average in this scenario, each person *should* control $200,000.

$2,000,000 purse ÷ 10 people = $200,000 each

You've already seen that doesn't happen.

Instead, after the 2 rich people get their share, $1.6 million, the 8 poor people remaining divide the leftover pool of less than ½ million dollars, $400,000.

$400,000 leftovers ÷ 8 people at the trough = $50,000 each

They're only getting 1/4th the amount you might expect, a mere $50,000:

$50,000 ÷ $200,000 = 1/4th

So if 80% of the people are getting $50,000...

What is "average" is NOT 10%, or $200,000 –

"Average" is only 2.5%, only $50,000.

Want a real fact that's even more *brutal*?

When it comes to money, statisticians and Peter Drucker tell us that the Pareto phenomenon really figures out to a 90/10 ratio. That is, a mere 10% of the people control 90% of the wealth, while the massive 90% of the people are slinging it out for the remaining 10%.

Running the same calculations as above, a $2 million dollar purse and 10 people, and applying the 90/10 principle, the rich enjoy **$1.8 Million dollars apiece**, while each of the poor folks only gets $22,222. Each rich person has 81 times more personal resources than each poor person! Indeed, these figures do more closely approximate the truth of society as you see it... But it's too hard to talk about this reality in a public forum...

Oh, and the rich? *Believe it!* Don't worry about them. They're not worrying about you! They're too busy *enjoying* <u>1,600%</u> *more* than <u>you</u> have!

$$\$800,000 \div \$50,000 = 1,600\%$$

Look at the houses, the cars of the rich. The million dollar stock market accounts. The international travel, the schools their children attend... Their overall enjoyment of life. If you're "average," you already see the difference in neon!

The myth of being average is a grand deception that's been foisted upon you!

Chances are good, as a reader of this book, you already know how insufficient $50,000 is to live a good life with your family while simultaneously preparing for your inevitable future. That's the problem, isn't it?

But $800,000?!! Now *that's* a different story! An elegant solution!

So we continue...

Running With The 20% Pack

We've already hinted at this... There's so much power in this secret that it can literally transform your life! Here it is, so subtle you'd better brace yourself to hear it! But *first!*

Thought Experiment: Who do you think is having more fun? The man with his wife on a Caribbean cruise, both of you with romantic eyes under the breathtaking moon as the ship cuts the sea, or the man who's back at the construction site, or bank or grocery, or assembly line working late, whose wife is working too, keeping children or stuffing envelopes because she *has* to?

Ah-ha!

Money is only one of the rewards success brings. Actually, barring some distorting factors, a multitude of rewards all come flooding in Pareto's proportions, too. 20% of the people enjoy 80% of the emotional satisfaction in this world.

On the other hand, 80% of the people pick up the cigarette butts of life on the sidewalks of despair.

Your Success Is Your Own Decision

When it comes right down to it, your success is your own decision. I wrote this book for you who have *decided* that you must have success, and that nothing short of death shall deter you from its bounty. You passed that initiation on your own.

You are welcome to the next further secret. Once you decide you will have success, then you mindfully search for the best opportunities. Perhaps this is where you are now... Your opportunity will always in some way have your uniqueness branded into it.

I have found direct response marketing – "mail order" – the best, easiest, most trouble-free, most liberating, business on planet Earth. I offer this book to you, to show you what it can do for you.

You see, direct response marketing is more than a money machine. It's a *lifestyle* liberator! If you follow what we've enjoyed so far, then you easily recognize that there's no conflict at all that this most lucrative of all businesses is also the simplest, the most no-brainer, and – because you pick your own area of passion to pursue. – the most *exciting* business in the world!

And you never go it alone! There are wizards who have been there before you. You can follow these wise ones and prosper. They'll teach you the principles, and whisper in your ear like a conscience when you err.

When you dare to make your contribution to humanity in a useful trade, bringing whatever ethical product to the market that wants it, you are serving the needs of human sustenance. Channeling your contributions through the direct response marketing of information products is the magic spell that will make you happy, healthy, and wise... Success truly brings the love, riches, happiness, and esteem you desire...

As Freedman Joe says,

> "I've been rich and I've been poor.
> *Rich is better!"*

The freedom of knowing your future years are sustained... Multi-million dollar bank accounts. Travel to Turkey, Switzerland, and the Galapagos. True love with your spouse, family, and friends. The independence to make the choices of your life based on preferences, and not because of old "have-to." Go where you want, when you want, with who you want, because you want to...

As one beautiful Puertoriqueña says it, it showers on you...

> *"Salud, dinero, y amor...*
> *y tiempo para disfrutarlo...*
> ¡contigo!"

✈ ✈ ✈

> "Health, money, and love...
> and the time to enjoy it all...
> *...with you!"*

By the way, though I'm a home-based business advocate, and most of the time assume your entire business is *direct marketing*, these principles don't hold true just for a homebased mail order operation. Direct response marketing, done profitably and efficiently, can be the basis of your whole business or simply a marketing pillar.

It's up to you.

If you're interested in discussing how I can help integrate a spectacular direct marketing operation in your business, call and ask for information on *marketing consulting*.

Think and Grow Rich

If you haven't read *Think and Grow Rich* by Napoleon Hill, the best advice I can give you is to get it immediately.

There are fundamental differences between the rich in life and the poor. They think differently. About themselves. About others. About the government. About opportunity. About failure. About success. About relationships. About God. And just as they have gobs more money than the average Joe, they have vastly more fun and fulfillment in life.

They think and intend in a way that causes results. The know that, unseen in this bright light, there runs an unbroken silken tie between feeling and the act... Between thought and manifestation.

Thinking with that profound knowing, causes wealth to happen.

Since you know this happens, direct your energies... From inspirations, into mindedness, to planning, to execution... into the reality of what you want!

This is what *Mail and Grow Rich* is all about – finessing that easy lifestyle in your own direct marketing business.

Though preacher Jimmie admits, "Simple... but not *easy*," I hear echoing the Hill, "*Think* and *Grow Rich!*"

So, running in the 20% pack?..

☞ You get there by *belonging*. Your mindset is the key... It's the way you *think!*

What you think, you do.

What you think, *happens in your life.*

Know that you must be rich. Tell yourself *how rich!* $100,000 per year? $1,000,000 per year? Do you want to live in an English castle like the once broke – but goal-setting – Dan Peña pulled off? What exactly *is* your lifestyle? When do you want this? Fix a date on the calender.

Embrace a philosophy of action, a philosophy of optimization and testing... Understand that the world makes no mistakes... Pay attention to the "feedback" you're getting to judge the success of your efforts... Then adapt with every step to achieve success.

At the heart of it all lies knowing what you want...

Mail and *Grow Rich!*

## Chapter 5

**A New Era of Opportunity,
Perfect for the 21st Century!
A phone... a fax... a computer...
    an internet connection on your desktop...
Technology makes it possible for *anyone* to
Run a *worldwide* business from your home!**

Announcing the World's Best Business!

"Mail Order"
in the
Information Age!"

My sole purpose in writing *Mail and Grow Rich* is to get you rich. Really Rich.

Some of what I'm going to say is going to sound complicated. Some of it incredible... Hang with me on the complicated stuff, because we need it to see how this business can instantly put you on a sun-drenched beach in the Caribbean.

The incredible part? Well, keep reading. You'll see all the proof you'll ever need to know for certain that it can work for you, too!

Information Marketing

The business you are embarking on is the marketing of *information products* through *direct response* channels – exploiting all the advantages which today's simple Information Age technology lays at your feet.

This is "mail order" as it's done today, in the 21st Century... not in the 1920's or the 1980's.

I can't say it enough. Reading is fine – it's *essential*. The error some people make, however, being so well trained in reading and analysis... is that they never *DO* anything with what they learn. What I'm saying is, that there's only one way to cross the gulf between where you are now and where you want to be, and it's not by being amazed by the stories of how good the direct response business is.

It's about being motivated, sure, but, beyond that, it's about *doing* the business. Offer a product. Do a mailing. This business is amazing! Do your reading and analysis, then move into action. Riches will sprout and grow around you all the days of your life.

This is the only business that *gives* you everything without taking anything away!

True freedom, independence, wealth,
time to celebrate life with your loved ones!

Let's get straight on one important thing right now. What we're talking about is *not rocket science!*

> Anyone can learn to do this business, even if you don't know how to turn a computer on! Even if you've never sent or received a fax before! If millions of other people can fax and computer, then *surely* <u>you can too</u>!

Today's "technology" is *simple* to use! Guaranteed, anyone can do it! Ages 8 to 98!!! ☺

P.S. That's an idea – have your kids do the "techie" part...

At a $10,000 per person marketing seminar in Los Angeles I was asked to share... candidly in a closed-door meeting with other successful business people, exactly what my own personal take on "mail order" in the *Information Age* is. Eager eyes took in every word, tingling with excitement!

What follows is a liberal transliteration of what I said...

Buckle your seatbelt, my friend, because you might think you're dreaming, and I wouldn't want you to fly out of your chair on this one... Though it *will* always remain a dream for the majority of people, *this success is quite real!*

And it's calling your *name!...*

"What Is It That Makes 'Mail Order' In The *Information Age* The World's Best Business?"

"This is the best business in the world because... Well... Where do I start?..."

"I'll just start *anywhere!*

There's literally *hundreds* of sound business reasons why "mail order" in the *Information Age* is the world's best business for anyone! Sure, this business shares many things in common with any business. And, in truth, the principles of running a successful mail order business are indeed the same necessary principles for running any successful enterprise.

What's different, is the group of unique and specific benefits that make *this* business – "Mail Order" in the *Information Age* – easier to start, run, and profit from than any other business in the world, while simultaneously delivering more passion, more fun, and more freedom in your personal life.

I'll try to live up to my responsibility to tell it like it is!

P.S. All the things the mail order business shares with other businesses? They're more easily and more profitably handled in the mail order business, also.

Instant Startup

What is it that makes "Mail Order" in the *Information Age* so rewarding? It is the instant startup? ...Because you can start the business in 59 minutes, and have your first order within 3 days.

No Money Required

...Or the ability to launch an empire with virtually NO money, less than $100? Or, that you can do it from home, with no employees, no overhead, no headaches?

Or because you can run it from anywhere, your bedroom in Boise, or your jeep in Costa Rica?

You've Turned The Tables!

Could it be because you've finally turned the tables on the insecurity of a j.o.b?. Or because mail order gives you wealth and independence, totally elevating your lifestyle, giving you both the money and the free time to do the things in life *you* like to do?... like travel to far away places, help loved ones... security for retirement...

Unlimited Income!

Or is mail order so rewarding because – and this is the important point – because your income is unlimited? Believe me, you'll find it very difficult *not* to make $100,000 per year in mail order... and it's easy to make *millions*! *You* decide how much you want to make.

Or is it because it's so easy to make money that you make money while you sleep, travel, and even party?! Turn your phone, the fax, and the internet into your own 24-hours-a-day automated profit machine.

Yep, I think so.

Many people search for any one of these incredible benefits. Any one of these could be the deciding benefit in your life... But *taken together!...* When you add them all together, there's an *irresistible* synergy!!!

THE WHOLE IS GREATER THAN THE SUM OF THE PARTS!

Lucky You! In The Information Age It's Easy!

The computer, the fax, the phone, and a copy machine – these are the essential elements of your savvy, inexpensive, and wildly profitable *Information Publishing-On-Demand* business in the *Information Age*. Talk about low level involvement!

If you don't have a computer and a fax, don't worry! You don't need anything other than a yellow pad and a phone to get started.

You can start with the fax at your neighborhood mail drop. No body needs to know the fax doesn't go directly into your "offices." Then, from your profits you can buy a fax and a computer. That's all you ever need to supercharge your profits in this business!

It's true, many people have done the business *entirely by mail* – and many people even TODAY are using the mail only. Some multi-millionaire marketers. But why?

A Worldwide Income

You're probably online. But if you're not, get on as soon as you can. Whatever your product is. The computer helps... With nothing but a $100 per year page on the internet I've recently snagged $1,000 orders from Rio de Janeiro, Toronto, Switzerland, London, Puerto Rico, and South Africa, not to mention Alaska to Florida, California to Maine, in the U.S. It's waiting for you. It's *exploding* for you.

A *worldwide business* – all from my computer and a telephone line out of my spare bedrooms! (My spare bedroom that the business has *bought!* I started in my kitchen in a crowded little two bedroom house!)

Even as we talk, we're exchanging email with profitable leads in Indonesia, Chile, and Perú.

It's the nature of the internet. Anybody who will get online can do it.

It's not too late to jump into the internet game. The pioneers have a lot of arrows in their backs, but you and I don't have to. We can jump on the internet and make money in days, not months or years.

It's the *best* time ever to jump on the internet!

But hurry, before the window of opportunity closes!

Why do I like the internet? One scenario. This is how I started... Assuming you have an internet connection, to start your business you only: 1) change your message on the answering machine to "sound like" a business, 2) put a free catchy classified ad up on America Online, 3) send a few craftily worded replies out, and 4) let the orders roll! It's that easy to start this business!

The Internet

*This is **the opportunity of the Millennium,** especially if you're just an "average Joe."*

*Because as long as **bandwidth remains tight** and for as long as the **search engines remain free,** you are on an equal footing with Microsoft. Really.*
- Ken Evoy

You may start directly with a web page. You can rent space for about $100 per year, like I do, or go to hypermart.com, bigfoot.com, latinmail.com, hotmail.com, or a long list of others to get all the *free* space you want. What other business can you *start* for *FREE?!!*

Register your site with the search engines like Yahoo, Infoseek, and Webcrawler, do a little newsgroup marketing, and the orders begin! It doesn't have to be complicated to be *effective.*

I'll come back to the internet again in a minute... But for now, I want to move on, because I don't want you to think that this whole business is about the internet. It's not – there's much more.

As a marketer, you're not really required to be an internet fanatic. Quite the opposite, you never want to get buried in the internet, but to *use* it... As you use a multitude of profit-producing tools.

Succeed In 1 Month

The mail order business is still so easy that the average guy can start it one month and earn $4,000 the next month! I don't know of too many other opportunities like that, do you?

One good ad and you're *running!*

Big Ticket = BIG Profit$

It's easy to get a good product to sell! But not only that, it's easy to get high ticket and *proven* products, with a *proven* step-by-step marketing plan for you to instantly cash in BIG, quick! If you're interested, I'll personally give you a high ticket information product of your own that can be the genuine beginning of your own mail order riches. Just keep reading.

Some people think it's hard to sell high-ticket products. The truth is quite different. The *worst* product we *ever* offered was a $10 information product. We had more people calling up and trying to barter or beg for the $10 product than we ever had for a product costing 100 times that! So our overhead to sell these folks went up! Imagine that! It was costing us more to sell a $10 product than a $997 product!

> **Advice to Those Who Want To Be Millionaires**
>
> *Find out what you love to do. Do what you love... Do something that you know really makes a difference. Do something that makes you happy in the doing as well as in the accomplishing. Do something that, when you're doing it, time stands still....*
> – Brian Tracy

Not only that, the return rates were significantly higher with the cheaper product. But the thing that bothered me most was the letters they wrote.

A man writing for a $1,000 refund simply says, "Process the credit to my Visa #4546-6654-5545-7899 (02/07)." Easy.

For $10 products the letters were looking like this:

> You must send my check today!! It's summer time, and the power company is going to turn off the electricity on Thursday. You know how hot it is in rural Arkansas... My baby has to have air conditioning. But I don't know how I'll pay the bill. But <u>hurry</u>, because my baby doesn't have any Gerber, and if you don't send my money I will hold you personally responsible for killing her because she doesn't have any food or air conditioning!

Of course, we wanted to send the money in an overnight envelope, which costs more than the entire value of the refund!

These types are filtered out with a more expensive product. That's good! You don't need this grief to make a killing in the mail order business....

Besides, people will pay for products in the $59 - $499 range quite readily – and that's where you have the margins to have profits! That's were the dream lies.

Lower costs. Higher profits. Less hassle. No struggle.

Handle with care cheap products.

P.S. As you know, any honest person who purchases *Mail and Grow Rich* receives a resale license as Bonus #1. That's a good start. However, if you inquire, there's more... Lots more. You can get high quality, good selling, *high dollar* products easily.

Your Odds Of Success Are 100%

When you possess the authentic secrets of mail order riches, mail order becomes like a big game you can't help but win! You change your odds of success to 100%, winning with that Mark Spitz advantage. (More about this *advantage* later.)

It Doesn't Take Much To Be Successful In This Business!

So, what does it take to succeed in your own mail order business? Well, in most cases, the people who are making tons of money in mail order have (only) 3 things going for them:

1. They sell **products that have a lot of profit in them**.

2. They have **a market that has money -- and that WANTS to buy what they're selling**.

3. They have the **right marketing materials** to communicate and motivate that market. (advertisements, press releases, direct mail letters, etc.)

You can have it all – everything – wealth, offshore vacations, bank accounts, Jaguars, multi-story houses, private schools, fame, respect, a secure retirement with no money worries – *everything* that *Mail and Grow Rich* talks about, and *more!!!*

Talk about "secrets of success"! Success is *this* simple! This is a profound truth discovered and *used* by few. You will learn how to activate all three of these essential facets to success – without stress or strain. It guarantees your success!

You can have it all!

There's No Discrimination In Mail Order

Age or ethnic background don't make any difference! Kurdistan or American, Venezolano, or Tokyon, you can get as rich as you want! At 22, 42, 62, or 92.

> Black, white, red, yellow, or brown...
> Pretty, ugly, or average...
> Mentally sharp or psychologically challenged...
> Male or female...
> Gay, straight, or bi...
> Tall or short. Dumpy or a rail...
> Running fanatic, bound to the chair...
> Early bird, or night owl...

Nobody knows... Nobody judges.

No Education Required

There's no training, no education, no experience required for mail order. Anyone with a 7th grade education can understand all you need to do this business!

No Expenses

You have no overhead, the #1 killer of small business. No fixed expenses that gobble up most entrepreneurs – inventory, staff, office or store lease, business phone, taxes...

You can run your entire business as a 1 person operation...

Everything you spend goes to *marketing*, which is what brings the money in.

Liberal Tax Benefits

Start from home, stay at home! Enjoy liberal tax benefits. Deduct part of your home on your taxes. Let your company fund your peace of mind. The business related books, computers, software, etc., you buy are totally tax deductible. The home-based business person enjoys loads of tax *benefits* denied to the ordinary wage earner. And they're all yours – even when you do the business part-time! Raise your children, enjoy your retirement.

Flexible Schedule

Because you're the boss, you enjoy all the conveniences of a flexible schedule...

Start From Your Kitchen Table

You can get started from your kitchen table... My 12 year old daughter licked, sealed, stamped, and mailed my first mailing list ever. Most direct marketing "organizations" have started this simply.

Start Your Business With A Roll Of Stamps

Most other "entrepreneurs" belly up with $25,000 up to $250,000 for a successful franchise. They've got their lives and their fortunes on the line. No wonder they hope and pray like hell they'll be successful, working 80 hour weeks.

Compare that with your simple startup costs of a roll of stamps!

A Proven Wealth-Building System

Most other startup entrepreneurs – faced with a very real 95% failure rate – feel insecure, scared, and frustrated. But because you're using a proven system that *works*, you feel secure and confident.

This Is *Not* MLM

Occasionally someone innocently confuses some other businesses with mail order. But, rest assured, mail order has *nothing* to do with any of the pyramid scams or the latest multilevel marvels. You won't be a shade dishonest or a pest to your friends and family. You won't be meeting friends at nighttime meetings or attending weekend rah-rah conferences.

"Is It Moral To Make This Much Money – This Easily?!"

Listen, I love to wake up, slip into my office, and find I'm thousands of dollars richer than I was when I went to sleep. It somehow makes the whole night better. Fine folks in different time zones, other countries, or people up late or early, have sent me faxes as I snoozed. I've made a great income while I was sleeping.

What makes it okay for me – and it'll do the same for you – is that I'm exchanging *genuine value* for every dollar I earn. Actually trading dollars for dimes. That's a good deal, isn't it?

Make More Money Overnight Than Most People Struggle For All Month

Then, after I've showered, eaten, and blessed the family, I tear back into my office for the orders waiting for me from my internet site. It just purrs along without my active involvement... I mean it's registered on the search engines and all... And I'm *thousands* of dollars *richer* – all while I slept!

But the action has only just started, because I still get the phone orders that came in and, for an afternoon delight, the mail at 1:30...

This can be *you!*

You Don't Need Any Licenses

You don't need any licenses to operate a mail order business. You won't have those costly compliance problems that restaurants, banks, and labor intensive businesses have!

You Don't Have To Endure Any Petty Office Politics

There's no petty office politics... Hey, you're the boss!

You'll like information marketing in the information age because money floods in ALL hours of the day and night on the phone, the fax, the internet, and in the mail! You just check your real mail, your email, and your fax; deposit those fat checks daily, and send the orders out... What could be easier?

Mail order offers a proven, reliable, dependable system to get rich quickly! All you're doing now is souping it up to do what the multi-millionaire mail order kings of the 1950's, 60's, 70's, and 80's couldn't do. Today, with the computer, the internet, and copy machines on every corner you can do in a few months what it took them years to do.

Plus, if you test a mailing and get a poor response, all you have to do is change the letter. Simple. Maybe just change the headline. How would you like to change a location or a decorating theme in a restaurant? See how easy this business is compared to a conventional business?

Pyramid Your Profits

You can start small and then pyramid your profits. For instance, if you invest $100 in ads, get 120 inquiries, and get a 3% conversion rate, you make $1,113.20 *after* paying for the ad. Look at scenario 2: invest $400, and you make even more.

	Scenario 1	*Scenario 2*
Money in Ads	$100.00	$400.00
Leads generated	120	480
Conversion ratio	3.00%	3.00%
No. of purchasers	3.6	14.4
Avg. transaction value	$337.00	$337.00
Sales Total	$1,213.20	$4,852.80
Profit$	$1,113.20	$4,452.80

But, want to see your wealth take off at hyper-speed?

Let's assume you invest all your profits, and then invest all your profits again in further ads. **Look at what you can do!**

Second Month

	Scenario 1	*Scenario 2*
Profits in ads	$1,113.20	$4,452.80
Leads generated	1,335	5,342
Conversion ratio	3.00%	3.00%
No. of purchasers	40.05	160.3
Avg. transaction value	$337.00	$337.00

| Sales Total | $13,496.85 | $54,007.62 |
| **Profit$** | $12,383.65 | $49,554.82 |

Third Month

	Scenario 1	*Scenario 2*
Profits in ads	$12,383.65	$49,554.82
Leads generated	14,860	59,465
Conversion ratio	3.00%	3.00%
No. of purchasers	445.8	1784.0
Avg. transaction value	$337.00	$337.00
Sales Total	$150,234.60	$601,191.15
Profit$	$137,850.95	$551,636.33

It's incredible how fast it can happen! I started with a *free* ad on *America Online* and pyramided those *profits* into cheap classified ads and then into bigger and more expensive media and direct mail. It's the perfect way to get started!

Most successful people discover that discretion prohibits them from talking or "bragging" about how much money they're earning. But Ted Nicholas, though a thoroughly likeable man, hasn't been shy about revealing his figures... He earned $400,000 in his first 4 months in this business. *This* is how he did it – pyramiding the profits from one ad into another.

Before all the shooting was over, he'd sucked in an incredible *$500 Million!!!*

You can do it, too! *Believe it!*

P.S. What if you shoot for the stars and *write* your goal at $400 million and don't make it? Wouldn't it be an outrageous event to have to adjust to only earning ½ that? Or ¼ that? Or 1/10 that? Could you live off $40 million? Crazy, ¿no?

"What Job Security?"

You have no job security.

Hundreds of thousands of honest Americans lose their job every year. Especially those 45 and above. Nearing retirement age... *Imagine that!*

If you feel more comfortable clinging to that little shred of security called a *j.o.b.*, start part-time – there's no shame in that. In fact, I would never recommend anything else. And then, in a few weeks or months when you replace your full-time income, quit.

There's A Lot More To Life Than "Business"

In the "mail order" business you have no geographic restrictions! You can **live anywhere – *in any location in the world*** – and do this business.

Equally as important, you're not <u>chained</u> to the location of the business. When you want to go somewhere else – for an afternoon, a week, or a month – just *do it!*

You are completely mobile! Most people don't think about this... but there's a *HUGE* difference between being "home-based" and *home-confined*!

Even when you "work" you are totally free. ...Any time. Simply forward your calls to your mobile phone (paid for with company *profit$*). Your son's little league game or your daughter's cheerleading... ...or a game of golf!

With Success, You Live An Entirely New Life!

Add a laptop computer to your technology array and you are <u>entirely</u> <u>mobile</u>! Get your important messages and faxes online anywhere in the world! Europe or the Caribbean, Latin America, Australia, or even deep inside Russia. Use e-mail to write a few replies. Make a few phone calls.

These are all <u>easily</u> <u>affordable</u> technology tools, <u>paid</u> <u>in</u> <u>full</u> <u>with</u> <u>only</u> <u>a</u> <u>few</u> <u>sales</u>. All the rest is *gravy!*

Because you have so much money, all kinds of international opportunities open up, even free travel. That's exactly what Ted Nicholas, successful direct marketer, is doing... I just received a letter he wrote me...

"I'm having the time of my life relaxing at my residences in London, Spain, and Switzerland, playing tennis, traveling...."

That's what "mail order" in the *Information Age* can do for you!

Experience the true quality of life that only money can give you! Independence. Choices. Boats, international trips, education, extravagances, investments, multiple houses, security... and above all, *love*.

You work in a clean, professional, respected, prestigious business. Never "work" another day in your life!

EXTRA BONUS: You have no wasted commute time. As a homebased business person, you enjoy the "8 second commute," which, over the course of a year, gives you an extra 12½ *weeks* of quality time in your life! Can you believe it?!!

Your Credit Doesn't Matter

Your own personal credit doesn't matter! Guaranteed! No matter what your personal credit looks like, you can quickly and easily accept credit card orders, even online – and boost your revenues by as much as 80%-120%! Spendable funds transfer automatically into your bank account. Easy to set up.

You Don't Need A Product To Get Started!

Believe it! You don't need a product to get started! Guaranteed. You'll get more exciting info on "joint ventures" later in this book. I've also written a course on "Mail Order" in the *Information Age*, and dedicated an entire module to joint ventures. They're simply the easiest way for you to get rich that exists! ...And if you're internet savvy – *affiliate* or *associate* programs are nothing but joint ventures!

Hang on to your hat, Baby, and your sunglasses, too!

Listen, you've already got your first joint venture going! Just by owning *Mail and Grow Rich* you have the license to sell the book – *even on a downtown street corner sales will impress you* – and keep a full 50% of all revenues generated! Not only that, but I'll be glad to give you the rights to sell several of our most successful products, products that everyone wants... And you can keep a whopping 50%

of all the profits! And, as they say in North Texas, with a $997 sale, "that ain't chicken-feed!"

Plus I'll show you how you can easily get a powerful array of profitable, good, valid, high dollar products of your choosing that you can start selling immediately.

You see, though I'm an advocate of having your own products, I know that the most important thing is to get going. Get some success under your belt.

First get your information business going, then develop or acquire your own product when you have more time, more money, and lots more flexibility. Then you'll get really *rich!*

When you discover the foolproof *easy* ways to create or acquire your own information products you'll never have to wonder again what you can sell or how you can get it!

Money comes in whether you work or whether you don't!

There's nothing I love more than taking a trip to California or Florida – or slipping over to Puerto Rico or Colombia – and returning to a swelling bank balance back home. In mail order, because your orders come into the order-taking service, or in the email, or over the fax, or straight to your mailbox, you don't even have to be there to get the orders!

How would you like to disappear for a few days or a week and still be packing in $1,000 per hour back home? All you do is make arrangements with a fulfillment house to produce and ship your product. Perhaps hire a competent secretary for a few of those $1,000 dollars? Talk about a *good* vacation!

By the way, I've got the coveted names, numbers, and addresses of all these contacts you need to do the business just waiting for you. *They're very hard to come by.* Stay tuned... I promise to tell you how you can get your own private copy of my very own "Million Dollar Mail Order Resources Rolodex" for *free.*

NO Accounts Receivables

This is one of the biggest problems of conventional business.

There are <u>no</u> <u>accounts</u> <u>receivables</u> in your mail order business! Nobody's paying you on account! (If you've ever suffered through a "profitable" business without sufficient cash, you know how important this is!)

You never have to wait and hope and beg for your own money! <u>All</u> <u>orders</u> <u>are</u> <u>prepaid</u> <u>with</u> <u>verified</u> <u>funds</u> <u>before</u> <u>you</u> <u>ever</u> <u>ship</u> <u>any</u> <u>product</u>.

Information Products Are Cheap
To Manufacture And Cheap To Ship

There's no product alive that's easier or cheaper to manufacture than information products. We sell $500 courses that cost less than $10. It costs less than a buck to duplicate a cassette tape.

Information products are **easy to ship,** easy to store. No problems with a warehouse, the corner of a room will do just fine. No headaches or special handling with shipping when a simple slide-it-in-a-wrapper and send it away will do.

The freight is cheap, because you also don't have to worry about any special packaging. Information products are practically indestructible, therefore they don't get hurt in shipping. Knock on wood, but out of the thousands of information products we've shipped out, we've never received one return for shipping damage.

And, get this, <u>your</u> <u>customers</u> <u>pay</u> <u>for</u> <u>all</u> <u>the</u> <u>shipping</u> <u>and</u> <u>handling</u> expenses! In fact, if you do it right, you can even clip a small profit off the shipping charges!

Outrageous Markups Get You Rich!

You know how I said you'd have to *try* not to make more than $100,000 per year?... Information products routinely take outrageous markups! You can sell products for $477 that cost you $6.18!

That's An Outrageous Markup! – the product only costs you a pittance compared to its *large selling value.* Compared with conventional standards, <u>your</u> <u>profits</u> <u>soar</u> <u>through</u> <u>the</u> <u>roof</u>!

Now I know, if you're past puberty, you recognize these markups as nothing short of <u>phenomenal</u>! That's the beauty of marketing specialized information. **Markups like these are the sure road to riches.**

Even At The High Prices Information Products Command, They Sell Themselves!

People *Want* Information!

They're The *Starving* Crowd
We Keep Talking About,

AND THEY'LL PAY *YOU* FOR THIS INFORMATION!

Simply Success

Some people think selling high dollar products should be difficult. Actually, it's a *LOT* easier. These products appeal to a credit card carrying group – they *have* the money, they have the easy ability to invest it with you. This means that expensive products are actually easier to sell than cheap ones!

People who want your product *are easy to find!* There are all kinds of relevant publications and *lists* that give you instant access to just the people you want to reach. **Target your audience** and you don't pay for wasted advertising.

The Ultimate Leverage!!!

Make no mistake about it, one of the greatest things about marketing information products is that you do your job once, whether it takes you a night, a week, or a month, and you continue to sell your product for years and years!

And everything thing you do – from sending out a direct mail piece, to appearing on Oprah Winfrey, to helping someone get happily involved with your product has *multiple consequences*. A sale is not simply a sale, but in itself stimulates *further* sales, builds relationships, and ensures your enduring business success.

What you can do is *incredible!*

Contrast that with working at the factory or at the office. You're *not* building your future, no matter how much they promote that delusion... After the last 2 decades, with downsizing, right-sizing, replacing people with 15-35 years in the company, drawing high salaries, with young low salary people... There is no security in the corporate world.

But every product you ever put together in your own information products business builds your wealth – immediately and for the foreseeable future.

Believe me, I *don't* like to work, but if I have to do it, I want to get paid 5, 10, 25 years for doing it. Don't you?

Only information products offer you this incredibly sweet leverage!

Publishing-On-Demand

Rake In *Obscene* 7,700% Earnings On *Someone Else's Money!*

Publishing on demand is the perfect solution to always having plenty of cash on hand! You don't even have to waste your money on inventory!

Most companies sink their precious dollars into inventory... dead inventory. If you were very frugal it could cost you $8,000-$9,000 to print up 5,000 books. (Bookstore books.)

But *you* can waltz down anytime – paying for the products you need with the customer's money, because he's ALREADY ORDERED and SENT YOU HIS MONEY!!! They run them on the high-speed copier, so 10 minutes and $9 later you're out of there! *Then* you ship the product!

What other business do you know where you can do all your business with the *customer's money*, not yours?

It lets you run your entire business with nothing more than marketing costs!

That's publishing-on-demand.

An Autopilot Business

The direct response business is a setup for an **autopilot** operation. All you do is place the ads, a lead taking service takes the leads, mails your irresistible special report to *interested* people, and an order taking service takes your customers' credit cards and notifies the fulfillment house, who ships the product. The order service deposits the money electronically in your account. This is *good!*

It's this feature of the business, plus, of course, the big buck$, that really give you, the individual entrepreneur, such freedom and independence.

No Selling!

You know how distasteful selling can be. Well, in money order you don't ever have to meet any people or persuade anyone in face-to-face contact.

Let ads and the mail to do the magical work of turning prospects into client$.

Your Income Is Unlimited!

Learn this secret, and the powers of fortune will sprout and grow forever! If you're not satisfied with your income, the solution is easy... and it's in your hands... and it doesn't take another degree or years of brown-nosing....

Just send more mail –

The more you mail the more you sell!

Literally, when you want more money, you simply run more ads and mail more letters! *It's crazy, but that's how simple it is!*

Your revenues, of course, cover the marketing costs of the ads, and put a weighty profit in your wallet, too.

There's a long list of people in direct mail consistently earning over $1 million *per year*, including Joe Sugarman, Tony Robbins, Ben Suarez, Russ von Hoelscher, Eileen & T.J. Rohleder, Ted Nicholas, Gary Halpert, Jay Abraham, and others.

Ordinary people....

And it can happen as fast as lightning! Ted Nicholas, $50,000 in debt, made $400,000 *profit* in his first 4 months, on a single product, without any backend. Robert Allen, struggling real estate entrepreneur, launched the "Nothing Down," phenomenon with a $20 classified ad and was earning $10,000 a week within 4 weeks. Jay Abraham has gone from being behind the 8-ball and near starvation to being the world's most sought after marketing consultant, able to fill a room with $1.5 millions dollars worth of profit$ on a single Saturday afternoon!

Residual Income

This business gives the ultimate boost to your financial destiny... Talk about leverage!!!

Produce a work once, get paid for it thousands of times over!

This is truly the *Lazy Man's Way To Riche$!*

You Get A Part Of *Every Sale* That's *Ever* Made!

When you write or record – or *commission* – a product of your own, which is incredibly easy to do, you're guaranteed to get rich! That's the beauty of information products. They're *intellectual property* which is strictly protected by the laws of nearly every country on Earth. People *have* to come to you! You have effectively *eliminated* all competition. You get a part of every sale that's made!

Your Income Is NOT TIED To The Number Of Hours You Work! Finally, put the magical powers of multiplication to work for you! This is the only way to get rich easily!

Earn Long-Term Wealth With A Firm *Backend*

Wow, if you think you can make money with a single product, the *backend* can make you *RICH! Backend* simply means *additional* sales. In mail order you have the perfect setup for a firm **backend** – every sale you make leads to *more* and *greater* sales!

It's easy to find programs with everything already in place, including sales letters, ads, and press releases, and mailing sequences, and products...

It's easy to grow your own...

When you sell a customer once, sell them over and over again. *Every friend is a friend for life!*

This makes a giant difference to your overall profitability.

Here's the *real* pleasure of a firm backend! I'll show you how you can make $100,000 a year with just 300 customers! I can even show you how to make $100,000 with just 1 customer!!!

Make money even while you sleep... and *party!*

It's ALWAYS great fun to wake up and log online, scope out the fax machine, and get the mail. *Money, money, money!* And it all comes without you even being there!

Sleeping, waking, or *partying* the money rolls in by itself!

It's 7:56 pm on New Year's Day. My Beloved, myself, and a couple of friends slip up to the upper floors of my 4-story estate, where my office is, to look briefly at something on the internet. At 8:01pm I hear the familiar cherished sound of that partial ring before the fax kicks in. And a slow whir-r-r-r-r-r, and there's an order on my desk! 5 minutes of doing *nothing but enjoying the good life* and another $782.00 comes pouring in! *It's a great way to start any year!*

The Newest "Millionaire-Maker" – The *Internet*

The Future Is Bright – And *Unlimited!* More people are buying more products and services every day on the internet!

The U.S. Department of Commerce projects that there are *over* 100 million people online – *today*. Others say 300 million. Some say 1 million new users a month are coming online. Some say 200 million.

They also are aware of the incredible commercial bonanza of the internet. Their projections are that sales – on the internet alone, not counting other direct response channels – will soon top the trillion dollar mark.

Thought Experiment: Folks, don't blink! This is not going to happen on some faraway intergalactic date. It's today, on Earth!

The most important location in yc town is on the internet.
– Jay Conrad Levinson

In a recent piece, *Success Magazine*, notes the billions that are currently being made on the internet, mentions some of the incredible projections, and addresses you, the reader:

The question is, what are you going to do about it?

Surely you salivate!

The Genuine Opportunity To Live Your Dreams

Sitting In Your Spare Bedroom, Your Business Spans The Planet!

But what I want to share most with you is, it's startling how easily you can harness the reach and sweep of the internet to draw in tons of profitable world-wide orders!

When you open up your own "mail order" business in the *Information Age* you've instantly got a *global business*. Imagine! A global business that you can start and run from your kitchen table. Your customers come from México, Canada, Australia, New Zealand, Switzerland, Argentina, Germany, England, the good old U.S.A., and every other part of the world you can think of!

You're playing in the biggest marketplace the world has ever known!

What that means to you...

In "internet mail order" you have an unlimited number of customers. Since, unlike a conventional business that depends on the surrounding population to draw their customers from, the *world is your market!*

All hours of the day and night! All across the world!

Incredible! This opportunity *never* existed before today! And what's so incredible is it's *not* rocket science! It's the *newest* millionaire maker, the internet!

Folks, we're talking about *billions* of dollars that American, Latin, European, Russian, Australian, Asian, African, and Arabian customers ARE spending! They're *looking* for things to spend their money on... Do you want to take advantage of a little sliver of their silver?

Open up your cyber-storefront!

You can do part or all of your marketing on the *internet* – which has already made thousands of people *overnight millionaires*.

Unless you've been living in a prehistoric cave (without television, radio, or any media of any kind) you know about the instant fortunes that have been springing up all over the place on the internet. Understanding the simple things these people did – and *still do!* – you can "copy" their success!

It's *easy* to get rich on the internet! Using the internet correctly, you almost have to try not to get rich not to get rich! In fact, according to recent research by ActivMedia, Inc., the average website is now selling $18,000 per month!

One of the greatest advantages you'll ever have is that it's *dirt-cheap* to market on-line! A full page ad in a major magazine costs from $7,000 to $50,000. Yet anyone can learn to market on the internet in a few weeks for the cost of a bag of Fritos, and make enough money in a few months to buy a Rolls Royce! Talk about comparing apples to oranges!!!

Get Rich Quietly

Minor success, judged by the media's mass consumer standards, translates into *major success* for you. It's actually easy to quietly, consistently, year-after-year, predictably pull $100,000, $250,000, or more per year from a low-profile lifestyle supporting mail order business. If you only sell 220 "courses" (valuable information product) you make $111,260.

And, hey, selling only 220 courses in a year's time is not burning the world up!

You don't have to do a lot of business to get rich! A "small" business of $100,000 - $250,000 a year can be a fortune for you, since you get to keep it all!!!

And it's obscenely easy to sell $100,000 worth of a good product!

In fact, it's easy to sell a whale of a lot more! You only need to sell 50,075 products at $19.97 to make a million dollars...

And if you offer the easy to sell highly desirable products we recommend, you only have to sell 1,357 products @ $737 to make a million dollars.

Think of it!

A few mail order sales and you have $1 Million Dollars!

Get ready for it!

Not only that, but your neighbors never need to know how you make your money. Not your neighbors, not *anybody!* You don't leave for work, you drive a nice car, you're always going away on vacation! "How does he do it?" they'll be whispering...

But, working within the walls of your house, nobody needs to know how you make your money. Believe me, it'll drive 'em crazy!

The Perfect *Lifestyle* Business

This business is *FUN!* When you sell *information, you* get to choose what products you want to work with. Like parachuting? Sell to parachuters! Like cooking? Sell – and talk about – a cookbook with your special recipes! Self-development, beauty, exercise, business success, investments, astrology... whatever interests you... these are the products you handle! It's a great way to stay jazzed everyday of your life – doing totally what you *want* to do.

> *You'll always make the most money doing what you most enjoy.*
> – Mark Twain

In the Information Publishing Business you deal with the things in life that you love so much you'd do them for free! Do you think the clerk typist feels that way about her job? Or the dirty laborer riveting brake shoes in a dingy remanufacturing plant? Or the teller at the bank, or the attorney in the courtroom? Of course [*smile*], you're not doing them for free, but for a handsome profit!

This business frees you for the lifestyle you *want* to live! You can do things that *contribute to humanity* or simply hang out at the beach, the choice is yours! And, as a prosperous, independent info-preneur, you can do *both*.

You may not want to make a million dollars. That's okay... You might just prefer to make an easy $100,000 per year and live in a cabin in the California woods. Check your mailbox once a week, ship the orders, make a few phone calls, deposit all the checks, money orders, and cash you've received, and be finished for the week.

You don't even have to be connected to any actual part of the "work" of the business – ever. In The *Million Dollar Mail Order Resources Rolodex* I give you all the contacts and resources for people to take your orders, ship your products, and mail you your profit$! *Like magic!*

But even if you operate the business "hands-on," since doing the business requires so little of your direct time – *how long can placing an ad or depositing a handful of checks take?* – you get to spend your time on the *quality* things of life – your health, your friends, your *family!* ...Your favorite golf course!

Yes...

Work Only When You Want

True security... that comes from the knowing confidence that you can sally out and make as many thousands or hundreds of thousands as you want, whenever you want – and sally back in, if that's your preference. Let me give you an example of just this approach.

The man who sells *Insider's Profit Matrix*, a course on making money in the futures markets, operates like this. An insider's view of 1997 may be instructive. These figures are available to any direct marketer from any mailing list broker.

He sold 4,243 units of his $43.95 ($39.95 plus $4.00 s/h) manual in the 1st quarter. Total sales of $186,479. Then he apparently went independent for a while, as direct marketers have a distinct tendency to do. His next sales came in the 4th quarter, I guess when he started thinking about the expensive Christmas gifts he wanted to buy his extensive family, customer, supplier, and team member list.

All he did was call his letter shop and tell them to mail more mail. He sold 6,626 units. Total sales of $291,212! Total sales for the year for mailing out a few letters, working only ½ of the year? **$477,692!** That's *just a few buck shy of ½ million dollars*!

And this guy's doing a lot of things wrong as a direct marketer. There were no offers for additional products. It's been 2+ years since

I bought the manual, and he's never written me once to try and sell me another product. (Although he does make a backend profit from selling his mailing list.)

In his book/product, he has no way to contact him – no address, no company name, no phone, no fax, no email address, no world wide web address! What if I *wanted* to buy something else from him? (A very real possibility, since there's always more to know about the market!)

People buy his manual because he has a sales letter he sends to a certain type of opportunity seeker that tells a convincing story that the material in the course provides an insider's strategy for increasing gains in the futures market while actually *decreasing* your risk.

People don't buy the manual from him because he's handsome or young. Nobody knows him. No pictures, no personal comments, no way to contact him. They buy the manual because they want the information contained inside.

You can do so much more!

What *Isn't* An Advantage Of This Unique Business?

Every time I sit and actually make an inventory of all the great things that "mail order" in the *Information Age* can do for you, I am amazed!

It really begs the question... "Why," I ask myself, "*what ISN'T an advantage of this business?*"

Break free once and for all from the low wages and measly appreciation of a job... Have all the money you could ever want...

Experience true freedom where *you* make the choices in your life you want to make, because you want to make them.

Enjoy a new level of prestige among your friends and neighbors.

...And receive love like you've never had it before – from your family, and from everyone who touches your life. *More importantly*, give love like you've never been able to give it before!

Truly, *information marketing* done *publishing-on-demand* style, using all the simple sales channels available to you today – like the phone, the fax, and the computer – can *FLOOD* you with money starting almost overnight.

Money gives you absolute freedom, great prestige, and a way to express love like you've only dreamed of before! Stop and think about it again... What would your life be like if you had money flooding in all hours of the day and night?

What if your biggest concern was incoming fax congestion?...

"Mail Order" in the *Information Age* can make you rich, respected, and free. It demands so little, yet it gives you so much. It truly is the World's Best Business.

And it's calling your name!...

Mail and *Grow Rich!*
$ ▲ ▼ ▲ $

## Chapter 6

The Principles of Wealth

True wealth is more than a big bank balance.

It happens all the time. People come into money, either through the lottery, an insurance settlement, or through some lucky event, like inheriting a thriving business from a rich uncle. And they run into ruin a short time later.

Why? Because, not having *built* their good fortune, they don't understand how to use it responsibly, how to keep it, and how to make it grow. Sadly, the greedy financial advisors, the party-crowd friends, and the obsequious relatives that sprout up with the dollars, do not give the newly lucky man any help. And he crashes.

A big bank balance is an event. You want a *life-time* of *assured* prosperity. The minded application of the principles of *multiplication*, *ownership*, and *leverage* will take what may have started with a few product sales into a multi-million dollar empire that can carry you and your heirs through several lifetimes of financial abundance and security.

As we get started, let's stop a moment and consider a profound truth of prosperity and wealth –

The only way you can get extremely wealthy is by discovering and implementing highly specific wealth-building principles and secrets.

True, it's a process, and you get better at it as you go along... That's the whole idea behind another concept we'll talk about called *optimization.*

The Iron Law of Business is that, for true prosperity (wealth that's immediate <u>and</u> that provides for you over the long run), you'd better truly *love* your customers. Because, there is no other way to prosper than to serve people. Sufficient numbers of people, in sufficient quantities.

Your business will take off when you make your first commitments to love and integrity, standing behind your commitment to making your prospects' and clients' lives better. Then your customers will return *voluntarily* to do more business with you, again and again and again.

As a *value-creator* you offer an authentic product or service.

So what if you've already got a product... that you're ashamed of? What if you have been offering a sharp and shady deal? Change now.

Any games you play with tricks, m a n i p u l a t i o n s, and misrepresentations may bring you a fast buck, it's true, but you've got to live with yourself at night. But even strictly from the crass, commercial, business point-of-view, you simply *have* to treat people right – *so they'll come back and buy more from you!*

> When you understand Francis Bacon, you do understand everything you need to grow rich quickly, and stay rich –
>
> *Nature, to be commanded, must be obeyed.*
> – Francis Bacon
>
> **P.S.** There are those who claim that Francis Bacon was the enigmatic Shakespeare.

Most business owners don't get it, but, it's basic:

• *You're dependent on other people!*

- *They hold your very fate in their hands – whether you survive, or whether you thrive!*

When you realize that, *you do have their best interests at heart*! What happens then, is that you operate with a higher purpose. <u>A passion</u> <u>to</u> <u>be</u> <u>of</u> *ongoing* <u>benefit</u> <u>to</u> <u>humanity</u> <u>motivates</u> <u>all</u> <u>your</u> <u>actions</u>.

There's great news here! It's about *karma*. When you have that positive *intention*, and you apply yourself with those efforts, quite naturally, the market responds. Everybody responds to thoughtful, helpful treatment, don't they? It's the Iron Law of Love.

Every time you make a sale, you can sleep well at night knowing that you have helped another human being improve their life.

If you can really improve your clients' lives, and you don't at least <u>make the offer</u>, you are performing a disservice to those people you could help, but don't.
— Joe Nicassio

The Ideal Product

This relationship announces the good news that every result you want is directly connected to certain actions you take. These actions are connected – unseen but measurably – to your mindset, values, attitudes, and ambitions.

This means that riches are a result. Riches are the *evidence* of satisfactorily providing a valued service! Paradoxically,

When you want to get rich, the proper focus is not on what you can *get*, but on what you can *give*!

Not on getting rich, but on delivering fruitful service!

The riches come.

In all our discussions we will assume honesty and integrity are the guiding standards of your operations.

And there's no business like mail order to let you maximize your opportunities to profit from them.

The Principles of Multiplication, Ownership, and Leverage

Introducing the first key principle to your fortune in any business...

Hear the drum r-r-r-rroll-l-l... Boom, boom boom!

Multiplication

To get really rich, you've got to put the power of <u>multiplication</u> to work for you!

We're talking serious, now. <u>Wages</u>, even in the form of <u>salaries</u> and <u>bonuses</u>, are what's holding you back! The irony is that most of the sheep in America firmly believe wages are their key to Freedom. (Good brainwashing job.)

Think about it. Just *yesterday* – not some day in the dim past – I read that Boeing laid off an *additional* 27,000 workers! It seems there's more economic turmoil in Asia. Indeed, there's always economic turmoil somewhere! I don't know for sure, but I'll bet these *were* some of the best paid workers in America. You know the stories, Bell, IBM, Boeing, even the wasteful governments (city, state, and federal) routinely lay off hundreds of thousands of hardworking, honest Americans.

And there may even be something sinister about it. Many big companies are going around the back door to slash costs. ...At *your* expense. New, younger people simply cost a lot less!

This morning's *Tennessean*, Nashville's metro newspaper, carried this stunning headline:

St. Thomas trimming pay, benefits of some nurses

St. Thomas is one of the largest medical employers in the entire Southeastern United States. Imagine!

But, oh how people hang on! The article says this move "unnerved senior nurses who thought a round of hospital budget cuts wouldn't touch those responsible for patient care."

Even the survivors can't breath too easy, knowing that they could be the *next victim!*

Yet, just to reassure those still standing, the hospital's official release on the "annual review of compensation packages" affirmed that these cuts are "unconnected to dozens of layoffs that began last week."

DOZENS of layoffs!!! Are we hearing this right?!!

Folks, these setbacks in the lives of the employees of Boeing and St. Thomas are just what I encountered off the front page <u>yesterday</u> and <u>today</u>. It happens <u>everyday</u>.

All this right-sizing (down-sizing) has been going on for years. You don't need convincing. If you're reading this book, you've likely felt the disillusion of the American dream. If the layoffs and the tragedy and the heartbreak hasn't directly touched you yet, you've seen and heard the stories of hundreds of thousands of ill-fated Americans who have felt the devastation. On a moment's notice...

"Job security" is a thing of the past. Only prayer, hope, time, luck, and a management decision stand between the timeclock and the breadline.

Not service, not time on the job.

Well, no thanks! *You don't have to put up with this!*

But more than the insecurity and servitude that go with a job, the sole existence of your job is predicated on the fact that <u>you're making someone money</u>. *More money than you're costing him!* Probably a lot more.

Now we're on to something! You have to be that business person to *really* make any money.

Quick multiplication lesson. Let's say your employer, being a wise and just employer only makes about $1,000 on you every month. (Just like breeding cattle.) Then, if there are 100 people in your plant and office just like you, your boss makes $1,000 x 100 = $100,000 per month. How much are you making?

You have to move out of the position where *you* are the one being bought and sold – *in a competitive market!* – to where you are the one doing the selling! I like to say, "You have to move to *PROFIT* to ever really get ahead."

J. Paul Getty just said "You *have* to be in business for yourself."

You have to move away from selling your *time* to selling some *thing*. There's only 40 hours in a week to work. Okay, okay! Maybe you can work 80 hours, but would you want to? And what if you don't burn out with that? Still, 80 hours – a brutal schedule – is an upper limit. But, even if you're putting in 80 hours a week, you're likely only getting paid for 40. That's no win!

If you're trading your "time," for wages or a salary, there's only so far you can go. You can't decide you'd like to double your salary in one year, and do it.

But you can in mail order.

For instance, let's say you get up the courage to go to your boss. And he doesn't take the occasion to fire you... If you manage to get a 10% raise, you've pulled off a blooming miracle!

> *If you are one of those who believe that hard work and honesty alone will bring riches, perish the thought!*
> ***It is NOT TRUE!***
>
> *Riches, when they come in HUGE quantities, are never the result of hard work alone! Riches come in response to definite demands based upon the application of definite principles.*
> *Not by chance or luck.*
> – Napoleon Hill
>
> ———···⋅⁝⋅···———
>
> *Riches are a result!*
> – Ted Ciuba

Contrast that with running an ad that brings in 6 orders per day – no matter what you're doing! You're playing at the beach, or coaching a little league game, or visiting with family and friends... Let's say you're making $100 per product. That's $600 per day.

However, you can always run another ad. Or 2. Or 3. Or 10! With 10 ads running, with no more work on your part (believe me, it's not too tough to place 10 ads a month!), you're now making **$6,000 per day**. *Presto!*

At this point, you shouldn't think that's too difficult. However, you just gave yourself a 6,000% raise!!! Which do you prefer, the miracle 10% or the fantastic 6,000%?!!

Once you understand the economics of mail order – or *internet order* – it's actually *incredibly easy!*

Multiplying Your Income. Earlier you saw how a mailing of 1,000 pieces earns you $3,813.57 after expenses. Then you saw how mailing to a million names earns you **$3,810,000!** You could do this inside of a year. But you could never earn that on your job, no matter how hard you worked.

And speaking of work, do you know it takes very little additional effort on your part to send out 1,000,000 letters rather than 1,000? In fact, it will likely take *significantly less effort!* Because, when you're sending out a thousand, like when you're first getting started, it's very likely you're doing it yourself, from your kitchen table.

However, once you graduate to 10,000 - 30,000 at a pop, you don't do these yourself. You have printers, lettershops, order-taking services, and fulfillment bureaus doing all the work for you.

Take that lousy job where they don't appreciate you and don't pay you what you're worth and shove it! Separate what you get paid for from the hours you put in.

> **To get really wealthy you must get to where you're earning profit$, where you can *multiply* your efforts easily.**

Mail order is a thoroughbred beauty! To make more money, all you do is mail more mail!

Listen! There's thunder! Here come the drums again... Boom, boom, boom! Roll-l-l-l...

Ownership

Ownership is the second great principle of wealth. True wealth comes from having your *own* products working for you... Few people realize just what a goldmine a copyright, trademark, or a patent can be. It's the *ultimate LEGAL monopoly!* When people want the product you provide, they *have* to come to you!

You get paid a part of every sale that's made! Anywhere. Anytime. It's not that hard to do with information products. Make sure you copyright everything you ever write or record.

Actually, simply by the act of creation you earn the protection of a statutory copyright. However, when you register your work for a few bucks, you've got a record for the world to see. But whether you register your work or not, it's legal and good to include the standard 3-piece copyright notice on everything you write or record: the word *Copyright* or the symbol ©, your name, and the year. Like this:

© Parthenon Marketing, Inc. 2001

I don't have the space here to go deeply into the copyright subject, but I treat it in depth elsewhere. The Library of Congress has details and actual forms that you can print off the internet with your Adobe reader. If you don't have Adobe installed, you can even get it free. It's all at:

http://lcweb.loc.gov/copyright

P.S. While we're talking about good government sites for information marketers, you really can't miss this helpful presentation on direct mail! Surf over to the U.S. Postal System's *direct mail* site at:

http://www.uspsdirectmail.com/home4.html

The advantages are clear. Your own products will give you more ways to make money, such as licensing others to sell your products as well, as well as create more prestige and credibility for yourself, thereby further enhancing your career and the money you make. When you talk about *ownership*, however, it's important to recognize one GIANT exception to the rule. Always,

Ready, Fire! ...Aim...

It's better to get started, with anything, than it is to wait until you've got things "right"!

You should consider heavily, for instance, about delaying getting started in direct response marketing, for example, to finish your own book... Because that could take a year or more! The most important thing is always, *get started!*

Duplication rights and *resale rights* to proven products can be the perfect way to get started. Then fill the gap with your own products, while you've got business coming in the door.

Duplication rights, also called reprint rights, give you the license to duplicate and sell a product. Sometimes you can find a good under-promoted information product like this for less than $250. Lots of mail order entrepreneurs have gotten their start this exact way.

Parthenon Marketing offers you several very lucrative duplication rights packages. If you're interested in getting free literature on these programs, surf up to http://www.mailandgrowrich.com or send us a fax requesting "info on duplication rights." It's free, and it can make you a fortune.

The greatest thing about duplication rights to hot, proven products, is that you NEVER pay any royalties, fees, or profits to anybody! Unlike a joint venture with resale rights, where you might be paying out 25%-60% of every sale you make, you keep 100% of everything!!

Resale rights give you the license to resell a product – but not to duplicate it. You get the duplication rights to the marketing *copy*. So you end up selling products you don't even have!

Hey, don't retailers wish they could sell products they don't even have in stock?!!

You send out the sales letter. Or put a version of it up on your web site. Then, after you've received the customer's money and deposited it in your bank account, you simply fax your product supplier (joint venture partner) a note to ship the product out to your customer. Like a $1,437 product... Or a $997 product...

45 days later you send them their deeply discounted 33%! You get to keep all the money for 45 days before you even have to pay for the product you got paid for! *Yumm-m-mm!*

So, the most important thing is, *Get started!* Then move as quickly as your success will fund it into creating or commissioning your own lucrative information products.

By the way, you can get a great book written for you $5,000, and that ain't spit when you're rockin!

If you're interested in product development and acquisition, Parthenon Marketing offers a great book, *How To Get Your Own Million Dollar Product*, which covers the subject in great detail, including copyright info. I'll tell you about this book later.

Pa-dum, pa-dum, r-r-r-roll-l-l-l... Ta, ta, tat!!

Announcing! The third great principle of wealth building...

Leverage

Those who engineer leverage into their lives and activities become exceptional beings, and legends in their own time.

Leverage has two interesting aspects... First, you want to maximize the impact you get from every single action, in and of itself. For example, when you write a sales letter, you'd rather have it bring in 600 sales than 50. We call this *optimization*. There's an easy way to do this.

Second, you want to make sure that every individual sale, act, or process integrally connects to every other sale, act, or purpose. Wheels churning within wheels, all acting in the present moment, all aiming at and moving toward some greater tomorrow...

To do this, you need to design a strategy that takes maximum advantage of the principles of wealth and to amp up each strategy to its max, so that it delivers the greatest payoff it's capable of. Wheels within wheels. Towers built on towers.

It's time to get into the realm of...

Parthenon Marketing

Around here we call this strategy and effort to harness these exponential powers of leverage *Parthenon Marketing*. It's simply to *establish many optimized "pillars of income."* Strategically designed and tested upsell, resell, and cross-sell *backend* opportunities in your mail order business (or *any* business) that *make you a fortune!*

Optimization

There's lots of unsuccessful business people, including direct marketers. You see, it's *NOT ENOUGH just to play the game.* The difference shows up in your commitment to WIN. The good news is that anybody can accomplish business success... It's in your power.

As a person committed to creating financial wealth in your life and business, you've decided you'll be a *passionate optimizer!* Why? Well, you've already decided that you'll make a fortune, haven't you? So how are you going to do it? The only way open to you is in how you use *differently* the same things that everybody else has to use, also.

Everybody has a product, marketing, advertising, and company processes. Today everybody has a computer and the internet. But your product, your marketing, your advertising, and the processes of your company yield greater results.

> *Your goal is to optimize and leverage everything you do... every dollar you spend... every customer you bring in... every resource you have... every effort you've formerly extended and can reclaim... over and over and over again.*
> – Jay Abraham

Why? Because you're always tweaking them. And replacing the old with new methods that have *proven* themselves to work better.

Optimizing, or moving toward maximizing performance, is like climbing a continuous ladder of improvement.

The way to get this high performance out of the elements and tools at hand is to measure the different sales processes (and all others) you implement, evaluate the results, and adopt the ones that improve your profit picture.

It can be as simple as paying attention. You make a minded experiment in some aspect, and if things get worse, you've learned that route doesn't work. If things get better, you've found your new standard, and you implement it into your life and business.

Witness the cake...

Everything Is A Process

Action – Reaction
Effort – Result
Sow – Reap

It's as simple as that. It applies in every part of our lives, even something as simple as a recipe...

"Momma, why does this cake taste so funny?"

"Well, Sweetheart, I ran out of regular sugar so I used brown sugar."

"Yuck!"

It really is a very deterministic world. Alter the steps of any process, and you'll surely get a different result. This is the basis of optimization.

Now, if you were baking a cake, and brown sugar made it taste *better*, next time you'd use brown sugar on purpose, wouldn't you? Well, if you send out two versions of a sales letter, with different headlines, and one pulls 9 times the orders of the other, what'cha gonna do?

Even *Hee-Haw*'s "Dummy-at-Large" gets a star on this question. Send out the better letter, right?

Unlike the brown sugar accident, direct marketers *experiment* with different variations of headlines, bonuses, and offers to *purposefully* find that winning combination.

Something more to think about... You never know how high you can go!

The truth about the risks in mail order.

Some have said that it takes courage to "experiment." They only say this from a profound misunderstanding of the truth...

So this is a good time to talk about failure. *What are the risks?* Well, I have news for you! *There aren't any!* Not practically speaking.

Kind of... Well, in a way... Well, I'm sorry, you see, I haven't been completely honest with you. In fact, there *are* risks. *BIG* risks.

The biggest risk is that you won't risk – because, paradoxically, *then – when you do not act –* is when you actually risk failure most!

You see, the *investments* you make as *tests* you would be making *anyway!* If you're going to send out 2,000 letters, it's going to cost you a specific amount. What if you change the headline on 1,000 of the letters? That won't cost you much, if anything at all. (By the way, as with all statistical principles, the larger the numbers in your test, the more reliable your results are.)

Yet you'll have the opportunity to see one that dramatically outperforms the other. I've written a lengthy special report on nothing but headlines, *How To Dream Up Hundreds Of Your Own Multi-Million Dollar Headlines.* There you'll see several instances where one headline outpulls another by 200%, 300%, 900% and even more!

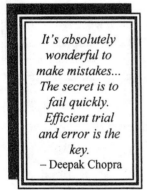

It's absolutely wonderful to make mistakes... The secret is to fail quickly. Efficient trial and error is the key.
– Deepak Chopra

This report gives you the *exact* words to use, words proven in *billions* of dollars worth of tests to sell any product. Stay tuned and I'll reveal how you can get a copy of this $297 report for the incredible bargain of... *FREE!* Fair enough?

"So," you might ask, "if you're teaching me all the proven tricks of the trade to up my response, why do I need to test? Why don't I just write a sales letter using all the principles, techniques, and words you're teaching me, and slam a homer with that?"

That's a good and a valid question.

Sure, you *do* want to build with proven successful ideas, strategies, products, and copy. But the reality of the matter is that no one can accurately predict what will happen. There are principles, but every specific situation, though operating within the principles, is unique and variable. But, if you'll spend a few well-managed dollars to drop a test or two...

The market will tell you!

As an example, you tell me, which of the following headlines scooped in the most money?

**"The Secret to Becoming a Millionaire
Is Simply Using the Right Words!"**

or

**"The Secret to Earning Millions
Is Simply Using the Right Words!"**

The man using them both, Ted Nicholas, was obviously testing to boost response.

You purposely try different variations, not to experiment to find failure, but success! The feedback is what you use to guide you to riches. Rather than guess wrong, you try out several alternatives, seeking to find, and continuing to use *and improve upon*, the most profitable variation.

> *When you test something
> and you know you have
> a winner –
> there's no risk involved!*
> – E. Joseph Cossman

That winner makes it all worthwhile. Just test conservatively, so you can't get hurt, then, when you've got a winner, roll out big!

What's just happened is that by testing, you've eliminated ordinary risk. *There is no risk.* You didn't go out and bet the farm you were right. You asked the market place by way of making your offer and then watching the results. Only on the security of good numbers did you roll out.

> *Mail order allows business
> owners to tirelessly, relentlessly,
> and inexpensively make their
> best, most compelling, most
> powerful cases without ever
> deviating from their rehearsed
> sales pitch, without ever getting
> cold feet, without ever forgetting
> an important point, without ever
> flinching when a customer gives
> them a difficult retort,
> countering every objection, and
> delivering the perfect close.*
> – Jay Abraham

Now you're not betting against the odds of mail order success. You've got a proven winner! Your success is certain. Fire up and mail more mail!

This optimization principle has taken many a man from rags to riches... It's smart business. Pure *leverage*!

Gary Was A Normal Guy

Gary Halbert started with a product idea, and the certain knowledge that other small frankfurters before him had succeeded BIG *overnight* in mail order. He *knew* he wasn't breaking new ground...

In his case, he did a mailing and received results. But he did not cancel the project calling it a failure. This is what the ordinary person might have done. *"I tried mail order once, and it didn't work..."*

It was not a failure.

Gary himself will tell you his story. He starts with a question, and ends with a statement of true grit:

> What should you do if your test mailing does not get good (profitable) numbers? It's up to you. What I did is, I tried over and over until I got it right. Where do you get the money? I got it by not paying my rent and not paying my gas, electric, and water bills. (I'm serious.) You know, it gets down to a very simple truth...

You Either *Will* Or You
Won't Do What You
Have To Do!

He changed different elements of the mailing, until he hit. And, boy, did he hit bigtime! It was his famous "coat of arms" letter. Some people say it's earned over $700 *million!* Others' place it well over $1 billion. Even Gary doesn't know for sure. (He sold the rights to a company which doesn't "brag" about their results.)

But, that's not all. The numbers are so big it's like the "Over 99 Billion Served" sign you see at McDonald's. It's hard to visualize that kind of money. Also, like that sign, the figures' growing every day!

With slight modifications – *optimized*, remember! – *they're still mailing this letter!* To the tune of *millions* of dollars EVERY YEAR!

P.S. Later when I talk about the 2 greatest salesletters in the world, *this is one of them!*

What other business offers you this kind of leverage?

Gary has become pretty good at this process, doing it over and over again. Anytime he feels moved to it, he writes a new letter and does a test mailing. He then rolls out to the tune of a quick millionaire's fortune.

As Gary says it:

You Are Always Only One Good Sales Letter Away From Having All The Money You Need!

What if Gary hadn't *risked?* What if, after one meager mailing he'd confirmed his suspicions that this mail order stuff was all a rip off, and that the only people who get rich in mail order are the people telling others how to do it?

He's earned *hundreds of millions!* Of course, he could have played it safe and kept his j.o.b. Heck, after all this time, he'd be up to $45,000 by now! ...Yikes! I just remembered! With his personality, he'd have been fired a dozen times... If he'd depended on the establishment he'd be *homeless* now!

True!

Indeed, the greatest risk is not risking.

Can you risk *that?*

Optimization In A Single Mailing

Now let's take a look at the results of a single mailing.

When you decide to market like a professional, you'll discover that the easiest things to test – and the *most effective* – are the design/teaser copy on the outside of the envelope, the headline of your sales letter, and the type of guarantee and bonuses you offer. These are your greatest leverage points.

Any one of these individual items can dramatically alter your returns. Together, the results are *exponential!*

Look closely at the following figures to see how optimizing the different elements of your sales letter can boost your returns. These are relatively modest figures. Let's say your optimized teaser raises response by 25%, the headline by 70%, the guarantee by 50%, and the bonus by 120%. Each of these improvements in and of itself is significant.

However, when you measure the effect of all four of these factors working together, you see you've ended up with a supercharged synergized <u>600%</u> <u>increase</u>!

	Control	Teaser	Headline	Guarantee	Bonuses
Improvement		125%	170%	150%	220%
# of Letters	10,000.00	10,000.00	10,000.00	10,000.00	10,000.00
Response	5.0%	6.2%	10.6%	15.9%	35.1%
# of Orders	500	625	1,062	1,594	3,506
G. Profit	$207.04	$207.04	$207.04	$207.04	$207.04
Total	**$103,520.00**	**$129,400.00**	**$219,980.00**	**$329,970.00**	**$725,934.00**

- (Starting with an initial 5% response rate on 10,000 letters, with $1.69 profit per letter mailed)

From $103,520 to $725,934

These fantastic differences are *easily* achievable – going from $103,000 to $725,000. *Exponential gains* from the combined effects of optimizing key leverage points.

So there you have it... My "confession" that there *are* risks – and that the biggest risk you'll ever run is not risking. Another paradox. It meant a career in the case of Gary Halbert, a life, prosperity instead of failure. It meant $622,414 on a single mailing of 10,000 pieces. It can mean the same thing for you.

Truly one of the greatest things about the direct response marketing business is that you *leverage* all these additional dollars out of the same finite investment in printing and postage.

You get these differences with *NO* additional expenses, taking *NO* additional risks!

It's *leverage* that *every* world class marketer strives to optimize... *Copy success!*

A Guaranteed Winner

Don't cheat yourself of the *vast differential rewards available to you*... Not when they're so easy to acquire!

Start by modeling the secrets of the giants. Then, when you write your own sales letters, copy and mimic their letters, their products, their offers, their bonuses, their style, their formatting....

Apply the same proven strategies the winners of direct response marketing are using to send your own sales into the stratosphere. Try several alternatives. *Testing* is the refining process. It's by trying out several different models that you find the killer.

Call it your control, and continue testing further, always trying to beat yourself – into higher profits! Always, the best working letter is your control.

Always study your results. If something doesn't work so well, no problem. Either eliminate it or, if you think it just wasn't properly executed, clean it up, make the specific adjustments indicated by the results you did get. Scientifically make your "mistakes" as quickly as you can so you can get on to the *real* moneymaking.

The Parthenon Strategy of Pre-Eminence

Your eventual success is all a result of how you think about your customers and your business. If you think it's about making a one time sale and that's it, then I hope you have your crash helmet on. Just as surely as the Parthenon with 1 pillar could not stand, you're headed for disaster. Nobody knows the exact time, but you're an accident waiting to happen.

Optimization of a single offer or aspect of your business is only one of the

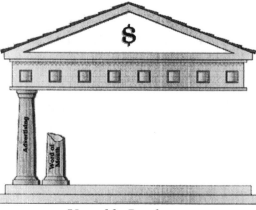

Unstable Parthenon
– Advertising, Word of Mouth –

crucial components in your game plan to build a profit machine that works for you over and over again. Your mindset, your goal, and your quest is to optimize *everything*.

For instance, let's apply the unstable Parthenon theory to your marketing. Most companies do some form of advertising. That's what they've been taught to do, and since it's so conventional, there's plenty of sales people knocking on their door every day. How *effective* that advertising may be is another question.

Further, though they probably don't do it actively at all, they may pay lip service to the true statement, "Word of mouth is the best advertising." Referrals.

The Parthenon Strategy of Pre-Eminence assures you, that's not enough!

That's another *great thing* about Information Marketing. It offers you the ability to make repeated and *larger* sales for as long as you want to market... People are prone to developing relationships, and, if you treat them right, once you've served them once, you actually have a *far better* chance of doing repeat business with them than you ever had of doing business with them the first time. Remember the *Info Junkie?..*

Congratulations! When you multiply and optimize your channels of sales and the number of products you offer your client, you multiply your sales. Actually, it's more correct to say that when you start applying these principles, you *exponentialize* your sales! *Line your pockets with gold!*

Your business will be stable when you have *multiple pillars of income* supporting your business. Just as the Parthenon, with many pillars, has stood the test of millennia, your business will become stable and enduring when you have multiple pillars of income – of several classes – supporting your business, earning you income. That's how you assure your own lasting success.

In one sense these multiple pillars represent multiple products and multiple sales channels. Indeed, your success is multi-dimensional, and you should think of the multiple pillars of Parthenon Marketing as actually representing the optimization of many different aspects of your business. *That's Parthenon thinking.*

The Strategy Of Offering Multiple Products

Taking our Parthenon, we can imagine that each pillar supporting the building is a different product supporting our business.

Enjoy The Easy Money's In A Firm Backend

We're talking here about the marketing principle of a *backend*. Every sale you make should be designed to make another. No product is an end in itself. You sell a $19 book to get your story out. Then, it's easier to sell a $337 course by mail. After they've been fascinated, charmed, educated, and regaled by you, and received genuine value, they then need further supplies or, perhaps, a $2,227 seminar. Perhaps some consulting.

Your mission, should you choose to accept it, and become exceptionally rich, is to always have various and more high priced products that people can use to improve their lives – thereby maximizing the dollar value of every single customer to you. *Whatever* your business is!

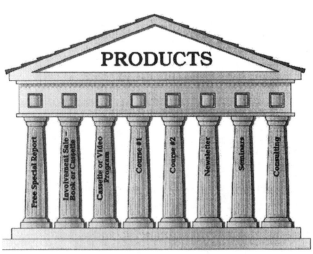

The Parthenon of Products
– Free Special Report, Involvement Sale - Book or Cassette, Cassette or Video Program, Course #1, Course #2, Newsletter, Seminars, Consulting –

Ideally you've got a group of related and integrated products, so this progression flows naturally. Build from a handful of introductory materials and products a funnel into more expensive courses, products, and services. Your constant quest is to increase the dollar transaction value of every sale, as well as to encourage your customers to buy from you repeatedly, so that you also make more over the long run.

And buy from you they will! *But they have to be asked.* But that's okay, because that's what you do as a marketer. You are someone who provides opportunity to interested people.

To illustrate, I'll give you a few ideas from one backend system I know well, that of Diversified Resources, Inc.

Our first efforts at building the backend sales occur right on the order form – called an *Enrollment* Form – with the offer of discounts for the higher dollar purchases. Here's the pricing structure.

I:	$ 97 – no discounts
I & II:	$337 – 10% discount
I, II & III:	$737 – 15% discount plus BONUS website

The same order form that offers the $97 product offers the $737 product. Which would you rather have?

We sell 400% *more* I, II & III bundlings than we do just I alone. Sure, dollar for dollar, it's a better value, and only the combo truly gives the ambitious neophyte notebroker the full complement of tools that will allow him or her to earn top dollar, but it's success is driven in large part by the bonus that's offered with course III.

This particular *bonus*, in fact, has made a phenomenal difference in the number of $737 orders our company has received.

I've put together a *GIANT* course on copywriting, one that, if you're interested, you can get for pennies... In just one little section of that course, 4 pages of *The Workhorse Of Your Multi-Million Dollar Mail Order Empire – The* Sales *Letter*, I show you the facts of a real, true, proven test of a *bonus*.

I ask the question:

Given the choice, **how do you get 100 customers to voluntarily send you**

$22,110

MORE THAN YOU ASKED THEM TO??!!

ANSWER: Give them a killer bonus!

This case study also perfectly illustrates the type of bonus you want. Something that *dramatically* **increases** the money you bring in, yet that *costs you pennies!*... Our costs in this bonus, to earn the entire $22,110, were less than $200.

Marketing Secret! The reason why this works so well is that the bonus has a high perceived value!

As you saw in the graph above, the bonus is just *on* thing. Your quest, of course, is to leverage *everything you do* to ever greater and higher profits! You'll learn *hundreds* of distinctions, each of which can make you tons of money, in *"The Workhorse of Your Multi-Million Dollar Empire – The Sales Letter."*

The *Paper Profit$* $22,110 Bonus

> With your paid in full enrollment in Parts I, II, & III you also receive our "pull out all the stops" SUPER "put you in business on the internet overnight" mega bonus, by itself worth over 3 times your entire investment in the course! It's our copyrighted *turnkey* world wide web presence. We build you a *customized* set of world wide web files. You'll instantly have your own homepage with your name, address, phone, fax, and email address on it. It will be your Note Presence on the internet. Overnight you'll have an audience of millions who can submit notes to you ONLINE! They work automatically, 24 hours a day! It can't get any easier than this...

You also see this upgrade offer on the order coupons of magazines, where you get substantial savings if you opt for the 2 or 3 year subscription. The publisher, of course, has just increased his dollar sale to you!

Continuing with the Paper Profit$ example, then, believe it or not, there's a free special report that rides out with every product delivery! No extra postage, it rides along for free! It offers the happy client, who promptly received his product, the chance to purchase a *related* product, a $187 supplementary product concerning For Sale By Owner (FSBO) note holders. 20% of the people who receive the *Paper Profit$* Course order the FSBO program within 2 weeks. It offers a genuine benefit to the beginning note broker.

A few days later, those who didn't take full advantage of *Paper Profit$* I, II, and III get a bonus opportunity to upgrade – and still get all the discounts and bonuses! (That is, if they upgrade within 30 days.) A good number upgrade immediately. Remember, they've now seen the product. They now know it's a quality product. They received it promptly after ordering it. They trust Diversified Resources and Ted Ciuba. The second order is *e-a-s-y*.

Then, in a carefully orchestrated sequence, they're invited to purchase a whole series of products, ranging from $197 up. Our best seller in the backend category is Ron LeGrand's *Cash-Flow Real Estate System*, a $1,497 product discounted down to $997. It's the best course – bar none – on making BIG MONEY, real fast, without money, without credit, and without partners in quick-turn real estate. Contact our office and we'll mail you out a hard copy *free*. Or, you can read the full special report at http://www.realprofit.com/cashflow

At every point these kind clients are also invited to visit our web site and see the wide selection of real estate and marketing courses we make available.

And there's special offers throughout the year, thanks to the fact that everyone who enrolls in the *Paper Profit$* Course gets a free subscription to the *Paper Profit$ New$Line*. We normally stuff a ride-along offer with the outgoing newsletter... at no cost to us but the printing!

Offer High Value Products

Be aware, however, that the future of your business is as closely related to the backend products you sell as it is to the frontend product. For example, we don't offer a bunch of real estate courses. We offer *one*. There is no peer to The *Cash-Flow Real Estate System*. Nobody who receives this product will ever be disappointed. That's another way of saying *everyone who orders this product is an incredible prospect* for the next offering.

As you'll see shortly, you can earn over $100,000 from a single customer this way!

Hm-m-m.

High Performance Profitability

These backend products give you the ability to leverage the value of a single customer. The very first act – giving a person a *free* special report, or a $20 book – is working on the final act – an ongoing customer relationship worth hundreds, thousands, or hundreds of thousands.

The first sale is the hardest sale! You've got to break through that very tough credibility barrier. Then, when you get this customer – *serve him for all it's worth!* We've got a saying around our company, and I encourage you to adopt it, too:

"Every friend is a friend for life."

Mean it. It's all about creating a lifetime relationship.

Design and unfurl a strategic, systematic, *profitable* backend with every product you offer. *How much service can you give to your clients?*

How To Sell At A Loss And Make A HUGE Profit

Just so we'll all know just how powerful what we're talking about can be, let's look at an example that Jay Abraham offers when he talks about backend. He had a client who sold collectible coins.

They actually sold their product *at a loss!*

Involvement Sale	2x Morgan Silver Dollars	
Sale price	$19.00	
# of beneficiaries	50,000.00	
Subtotal	$950,000.00	
Cost of product	$21.00	
# of beneficiaries	50,000.00	
Subtotal	$1,050,000.00	
Profit/(loss)		**$(100,000.00)**

A pretty substantial loss...
But let's look at the backend.

Backend #1		
Avg. per sale	$1,000.00	
Beneficiaries	10,000.00	
Sales		$10,000,000.00

Backend #2

Avg. per sale	$1,000.00	
Beneficiaries	250	
Sales	$250,000.00	
3x per year		$750,000.00

Backend #3

Avg. per sale	$5,000.00	
Conversions	1,500.00	
Sales		$7,500,000.00

TOTAL SALES YEAR ONE: **$18,150,000.00**

Let's Recap: In their advertising for these coins they "admitted" that they were actually selling at a loss, even based on wholesale costs! Everyone recognized it was a great value... And bought! To the tune of a $100,000 loss!

Some loss they took, right?! They wisely knew that it was really part of the irresistible customer-capture *advertising* costs. With the strategic deployment of a firm backend, they were able to leverage that initial customer acquisition "loss" into a gain of over $18 Million!

Get this! Each of these buyers had identified themselves as someone who understood something about the value of coins, as well as being a person who would purchase by mail. The *perfect* targeted audience for a backend offer!

They'd bought from the company, been pleased with the value, been pleased with the service. *Heavens!* You can't get a better prospect than your own satisfied mail order customer!!!

> *Success leaves clues.*
> – Tony Robbins

And guess what? A little literature went out with each of the 50,000 orders. Can you believe it? Another offer! In accord with time-proven backending principles, the company raised the ante. 20% of the original respondents responded to this second offer.

10,000 customers came back and ordered $1,000 worth of precious coins! Within 60 days of the first mailing, the company was showing a $10 Million profit!

Not only that, but even though they can't snag 10,000 orders every month, they do snag a steady 250 orders every three months from this same group of original buyers. That's an *easy* $250,000 every quarter. That alone is a million dollar per year revenue.

But, again following the natural progression of backend buyers, there are a select number of buyers who want *even more!* The company targets the repeat buyers and upsells them into a $5,000 precious coin investment. To the tune of *$7.5 Million Dollars!*

Total profit: $18,150,000 – From a $100,000 loss!

This perfectly illustrates the power of a firm backend!

P.S. Don't take this illustration as an indication that you have to sell at a loss. Or that you have to have deep pockets to be able to do business. What it illustrates is that it's not on the first sale that you make your money...

What it illustrates is the incredible leverage that's available to you by strategically working your own customer list!

– Bonus Insert –

"What Does Breaking Boards Have To Do With Your Success?"

Two volunteers came forward. A young diminutive girl broke the board with one clear stroke. The husky country man, after pounding away at it 10 times, crawled away – *shamed.*

What gives? Whether you can break a board or not depends entirely on what you "see." When you "see" the top of the board, that's where you stop – *ouch!* When you see the *space beyond the board*, you pass through it like it's cobweb.

It's not size, might, or even trying hard, as our burly friend with the throbbing hand learned...

It's not who you are by the fortunes of birth... money, looks, culture...

The difference lies in your *mental focus.*

You harness this same power when, *before* the day they make their first purchase with you, you see satisfied happy clients enjoying future products of your own.

You'll serve them well!

From a loss – ($100,000) – to a million dollar fortune!

You Make Your Real Money On The Backend!

It's generally not possible to make the huge income you want to make on just the front end. But the backend is your true front door to riches!

None of this is boring, hard, or challenging, but it is something that most beginning homebased entrepreneurs miss out on entirely, and therefore fail even when it looks like they're doing things right. It's crucial that you implement this key component of the Millionaire's mindset.

When your prospect makes their first purchase, there's a design, a chute, if you will, that encourages them – starting with that moment of their first purchase – to spend more money, and more money, on products they don't even yet dream exist. But it is your plan...

The Strategy Of Multiplying Your Channels Of Sales

The second major dimension of pillars you want to build into your business Parthenon involves multiple sales channels. Every direct response marketing company can make money through at least 8 different sales channels. I imaginatively assign one of these sales channels to each of the 8 pillars on the ends of the Parthenon.

As such, you can visualize your Parthenon Marketing strategy as composed of the 8 marketing pillars of direct mail, advertising, internet, publicity, backend, joint venture alliances, distributors, and a newsletter.

In practice, these are all interdependent, simultaneous, and multi-dimensional... all affecting and affected by each other...

In other words, you can sell a joint venture product through a

Parthenon Marketing
– Direct Mail, Advertising, Internet, Publicity, Backend, Joint Ventures, Distributors, Newsletters/E-zines –

combination of advertising and direct mail, simultaneously offering it on the internet, through distributors, and with your newsletter.

You know what we're talking about with direct mail, advertising, the internet, and the backend. But *publicity? To sell? Yes!* And what in the world is this "joint venture" and "distributor" stuff? *Simply the easiest way to get new products and giant new revenues!*

Publicity. There's always a way to make favorable publicity for your product. You can get rich for the price of a postage stamp.

Harold Moe earned $3,591,000 from a single feature in *Family Circle* magazine! Get on *Oprah* and you can accelerate that to a couple of *days!*

It's happened. It happens. It can happen to you.

Naturally, there are secrets to writing effective press releases. Ignoring those secrets *guarantees* your failure. This is where most people's efforts consign them....

> *Traditional marketing believes that advertising works... Or that direct mail works... or that having a web site works.*
>
> *Guerilla Marketing says that those are silly notions. Advertising doesn't work. And direct mail doesn't work. And having a website doesn't work.*
>
> *The only thing that works now are marketing combinations. And that means that if you advertise, and you do direct mail, and you have a website, all 3 of them are going to work – and they're gong to help each other work.*
> Jay Conrad Levinson

I reveal these secrets' depth and power in *Million Dollar Publicity Strategies That Don't Cost You A Dime ...and Make You Millions!* I'll give you full details soon on exactly how you can get this $147 report absolutely free.

Joint Venture is nothing more than a term describing an agreement whereby two companies work together to make a mutual profit. It's when you and I agree that you can market my course, The *Mail and Grow Rich* System, that I'll inventory and ship it out, and that you keep 50% of the revenues!

You can get rich on either end of this equation. Suppose you drop the proven mail piece we give you with your *resale rights*, and you make

$368,500? Did you make half of that, $184,250, last year? And you can drop another load of mail, can't you?

The majority of your backend products may in fact be joint venture products, as they are for us. We've got joint venture or resale rights to products from Bob Serling, Ted Nicholas, Ted Thomas, Russ von Hoelscher, Mark Nolan, Paul Hartunian, Ron LeGrand, Brian Keith Voiles, Kirt Christensen, and a select group of others.

I show you exactly how to set up these profitable joint venture relationships in *High Impact Backend Marketing*. This workshop normally sells for $197, but I'm going to tell you soon exactly how you can get it *absolutely free!* In the manual you get actual copies of <u>actual</u> joint venture agreements. Just copy what we do, adapt it to your specific situation, and you're rollin'!

It works just as good when someone is selling your products... Then, instead of acquiring the resale rights, you license distributors, so that they have the right to resell *your* products. Though you make substantially less on a per piece basis than you do when you're selling it yourself to the end user, the greater quantities sold more than make up for it. Plus, they were sold *at no cost to you...*

You don't actually *do* anything to make distributor sales. Your distributors do everything.

Newsletter. Then, you should certainly have a newsletter – even if it's free. You're talking to your own customers!... (Enough said.) Every issue has another special! And if you're online, get used to the term "e-zine." That's an electronic-magazine, or newsletter. You can read more on e-zines in *How To Use The Internet To Make Your First Million Dollars*.

How To Exponentially Increase The Value Of A Sale...
The Story of a Distributor.

We have a customer, Thomas Morgen, who made his first purchase from us on the internet a couple of years ago. That was a $337 purchase. He promptly brokered a few mortgage note transactions (the subject of the course... *yes, it really works!*).. Then we "let" him sell our *Paper Profit$* courses on his internet web site. The beginning of a greater relationship. The *ultimate* backend! One thing led to another and I recently wondered just how much he'd meant to us. Curious, I took just a slice of his business – the last 2 full years.

During that period Tom upgraded from level II to level III of the *Paper Profit$* course for $452.00. Then, doing all the work himself, Tom promptly earned us $4,812.60 in one month on a brokering transaction. Acting directly as our distributor, he then sent us $68,845.45. So far we're up to $74,110.05. But that's not all!

Some of the customers Tom brought into the funnel – at outrageous profits to us originally – have become <u>multiple</u> <u>purchasers</u> and <u>distributors</u> themselves. Total product revenues from his client base were $25,519.18.

TOTAL: $99,629.23

Analysis of selected "per customer" Profit Responsibility

Morgen

Paper Profit$ Course		$452.00	
Brokering Revenues		$4,812.60	
Distributor Sales		$68,845.45	
Subtotal		$74,110.05	$74,110.05
1st Level	**Humphrey**		
	Paper Profit$ Course	$349.00	
	Brokering Revenues	$15,754.00	
	Distributor Sales	$3,396.28	
	Subtotal	$19,499.28	$19,499.28
2nd Level	**Hansen**		
	Paper Profit$ Course	$782.00	
	Web Site	$1,137.00	
	Subtotal	$1,919.00	$1,919.00
1st Level	**Smithey**		
	Paper Profit$ Course	$349.00	
	Mega Mortgage Course	$495.00	
	InfoMillions Course	$309.00	

Misc	$129.00	
FSBO Course	$152.00	
Web Site	$1,137.00	
Distributor Sales	$1,529.90	
Subtotal	$4,100.90	$4,100.90

Grand Total From A Single Sale To Morgen $99,629.23

Can you believe Tom sent us that much money without us ever doing a single thing? Here you see *3 generations* of sales – Morgen sales Humphrey, Humphrey sales Hansen. That's the power of an opportunity-laden *backend!*

All this flowed from a single sale.

$99,629.23

And it's not over yet!

I guess you also can see why I LIKE the internet!

P.S. Oh, by the way, I've got a program wherein you get a fully functioning **web site**, with your *own* unique URL, when you decide to be really rich. If you'll contact us and request the "web site details," I promise to give you the blow-by-blow facts of internet commerce. Don't ignore the internet when it can be so easy! It's a cash cow!!

P.P.S. Next it can be *you*. What if you had 4 Tom's making you money like that? That's $398,517 per year for working a couple hours every day. What if you had 12 Tom's? **That's $1.2 Million Dollars.** It's *entirely possible*! These distributor guys will make you rich!

P.P.S.S. It sure is nice of Tom to *do all that work* and *make you all that money*, isn't it?

The Art and Science of Getting Rich

This chapter takes you on a high velocity reading experience. You've just been introduced to the 3 universal principles of wealth. Building your mail order business on *multiplication*, *ownership*, and *leverage* will assure you permanent prosperity. Abide by them, implement them in your business activities, and you will prosper beyond your wildest dreams.

Ignore them, and any success you have will be temporary.

Multiplication allows you to turn the tables on employment, where you break away from the insecurity and low pay of a job and thrust yourself into riches, independence, and prestige.

No longer do you sell yourself by the hour or the month to some ungrateful company who works you too hard and pays you too little. You work for yourself, offering a product who's revenues you can multiply no end. Finally, do what all the rich people throughout history have done. Put "things" like advertising and products to work for you.

Then... want more money? Simple, mail more mail!

You've got the perfect road laid out before you. Start parttime. You don't need to go fulltime until sales replace your regular "security" by *multiples!*

Ownership gives you the riches associated with an absolute monopoly. Anytime, anywhere people want the product you offer, *you* get a part of the income.

It's perfectly fine to *start* a business with no products of your own – and in fact, that's a very good way to get started. One of the *best!* But as you build your business and your expertise, adding your own easily created products – and it can be as simple as recording a phone conversation on cassette – you expand your profit base dramatically.

Leverage allows you to get the maximum bang for your buck in everything you do. Every single process, such as sending out a sales letter, is optimized for maximum profitability. At the same time, you have an array of different products bringing you money, as well as an array of different sales channels.

The best thing about it all is that mail order is the perfect "setup" business to implement these principles.

When you sell a variety of products, strategically designed to offer your beloved customers yet *more*, offering them through direct mail, advertising, the internet, publicity, backend communications, joint venture alliances, distributors, and newsletters you have money coming at you from all directions all the time. It's a good feeling.

Further, every one of these channels can be optimized to yield a greater return...

Parthenon Marketing allows you to capture tons of sales from other products and other sales channels that otherwise would surely go to your competitors!

You prosper, not for a season, but for a lifetime.

An Exclusive Invitation

There you have it all! Now you yourself can easily earn $3,000 per day or $3,288 in less than 1 hour. Or a lot more! All from home!

You've learned the secrets that will allow you to name your own price in the mail order arena, whatever that is. You've discovered the clear and easy principles that will assure your success.

Riches in mail order are the result of a minded awareness of what it takes to succeed coupled with drive and the courage to act. Success follows effort as surely as day follows night.

And it's never been easier for the average guy to do it than it is today... With the phone, a fax, your computer, and the neighborhood copy machine.

This book has been your invitation to join a very exclusive fraternity. The fraternity of the independently wealthy in mail order. It's now up to you to take the next step. You've now got everything you need to succeed.

Mail and *Grow Rich!*

$ ▼ ▲ ▼ $

...You've had a taste, and now you long for the wealth and independence that your own successful homebased mailorder business can bring!

This *BONUS* Section Reveals!...

Ted Ciuba, Marketer,
Marketing Consultant

"How To Unleash Your Own Million Dollar Potential!"

...more quality time with your family, a new car, a bigger finer house, the privileged schools, expensive clothes, fine dining, the travel, security for your future years, and the respect and prestige that come with success – *self-respect above all...*

Dear Profit-Motivated Friend:

You want to work a few hours a day, doing something you love, enjoying total independence, don't you?

So how do you unleash your own million dollar potential?

First, you should recognize that fortune and your own efforts have already come to your side.

You have now placed yourself in front of the greatest, most comprehensive, most simple-to-understand, and proven course that exists on "mail order." Especially if you're interested in the way it's done today, in the 21st Century, in the *Information Age.*

You're ready for The *Mail and Grow Rich* System, a course I designed specifically for you! This course can take you, with what you've already learned in this book, and immediately put you in the driver's seat of your own profitable mail order business.

You see, there's only so much anyone can put into a single book intended for mass distribution. But if you're truly ready to earn your fortunes in mail order, if you're ready to make that quantum leap from "reading" about good fortune to really raking in your share, then,

You're ready for The *Mail and Grow Rich* System!

Successful, savvy, in tune with the trends...

**Using Today's Simple Technology Tools Like
The Phone, A Fax, Your Computer, and the
Neighborhood Copy Machine,
Working Part-Time From Your Home,
You Can Quickly, Easily, Safely, and
Insanely Earn Well Over $100,000 Per Year in...**

"Mail Order" in the *Information Age!*

You've reached the point where you're ready to strap on your own electrically charged thinking cap when you think about products – recognizing that more important than having a "product" is having the *right product.*

And you're ready to unfailingly choose and promote only *killer* products!

You're ready to scribble a few simple lines, following proven formulas, to write a *killer* sales letter that sucks in so many orders that 2 armed Brinks men come to your front door for your bank deposits.

You're ready to level in eyeball-to-eyeball, working on a direct mail project with me, fighting the business battle with bloody hand-to-hand combat. ...Not laid back in vicarious oblivion in your wife's sofa watching *I Love Lucy* reruns and yumming over her soft yogurt.

The *Mail and Grow Rich* System is a rigorous course, a *tour de force* of everything you need to reach mega success in "Mail Order" in the *Information Age*. Not for the faint of heart!

By the time you finish the *Mail and Grow Rich* System you will have more actual know-how on how to be successful in business than 99.9% of the people on planet Earth. This is no exaggeration! And, believe it or not, even <u>95%</u> of *business owners* <u>don't</u> <u>understand</u> <u>what</u> <u>you'll</u> <u>know</u>!

The Mark Spitz Advantage

You'll be taking for yourself what I call the **Mark Spitz advantage**... What I mean is, assume there's a boatload of 1,000 people cruising the Mediterranean ... Assume that some government decides they want to sink that ship. Everybody who can swim 10 miles survives. Everybody who can't, dies.

Well, business life may not be so extreme, but it sometimes is a matter of survival under adverse circumstances. Wouldn't you agree that the odds of failure for these once sunny passengers would be about 99.5%? That is, probably less than 5 of the 1,000 people would make it to shore. Yep, 995 die.

Now further assume that Mark Spitz, winner of 9 Olympic gold medals in swimming, were on that boat. Sure, the odds of failure are 99.5%. But, for Mark Spitz... the "odds" simply don't matter. They're not part of the game he plays... Assuming that same benign government doesn't strafe back F-18's to spike him in the water, Mark Spitz's odds for **success** are 100%.

That's the advantage having the complete *Mail and Grow Rich* System will give to you. No matter what the "masses" are doing, and *undoubtably the majority of them are failing*, <u>your</u> <u>odds</u> <u>for</u> <u>success</u> <u>stay</u> <u>pegged</u> <u>at</u> <u>100%</u>!

What separates you from the good life you desire is nothing more than *knowledge - secrets* the millionaires don't talk about. Secrets that you get in The *Mail and Grow Rich* System.

Announcing! ...It's all yours!

Get Rich Quick 'n' Easy...

The **MAIL AND GROW RICH** System
**Gives You A Realistic, Low Cost, Low Risk,
Complete <u>Step</u>-<u>By</u>-<u>Step</u> *Proven*
Mail Order System That <u>Anyone</u> <u>Can</u> <u>Use</u>
To Instantly Accomplish**

Financial Independence
Starting *Today!*
100% Guaranteed!

Everything that *Mail and Grow Rich* talks about?...
It's *here!*

This course gives you the disarmingly simple
inside secrets that allow *you* to operate a global
enterprise from your spare bedroom, leveraging today's
simple technology tools into a million dollar income.

Everything from your first product, to your full-
fledged marketing campaign that supports your own
multi-million dollar empire. You get all the secrets,
revealed by one who's *doing* what he's teaching.

You learn the inside secrets of marketing –
writing sales letters that *sell* and offering products
that customers buy *again* and *again!*

You get product templates, advertising templates,
and marketing templates. It's like connect-the-dots,
all you have to do is pull out your template to
construct a perfect marketing campaign. Follow the
checklists to make sure you have all systems *go*.

You only have to follow the guidelines to set up
your own autopilot marketing system in days, so you
have total independence, while money floods into your
golden vaults, no matter what you personally are
doing... Baking on the beach in Bermuda, hacking
through the jungle in Costa Rica, or appreciating the
opera in Milan.

Simply *Success* –
When You Want To Learn Something,
Go To Someone Who's Successful

Unlike a lot of get rich authors, I've done
everything I talk about. You've been looking at my
real-life examples. Sure, I've learned *TONS* from
books, videos, and audios – I'd be a fool *not* to be
addicted to learning and improvement – but there's
nothing here that I haven't done and succeeded at
before offering it to you.

More importantly, I'm *still* doing this business.
You're not learning from a man who's a legend in his
own mind...

Or a legend before your time... Someone who did
something that worked once, quite possibly because of
some unique fortune of the times, and lives on telling

the story over and over again, like a worn-out
veteran. That's the problem, you undoubtedly already
know, with the majority of get rich schemes in the
bookstores of America, Europe, and across the world.
Somebody had 1 success, wrote a book... and misleads
you.

Or worse, someone who's *only* written about it,
like a salaried writer! How could someone like that
possibly know what you need?

**You, dear friend, want to know how you do business
in the dawning of the 21st Century. With all the
incredible new advantages that are yours!** *That's* **what
you'll find inside the walls of the vaunted** *Mail and
Grow Rich* **System.**

You Can't Learn This Valuable Knowledge
Anywhere Else

Unless you've been living in a prehistoric cave
(without television, radio, or any media of any kind)
you know about the instant fortunes that have been
springing up all over the place on the internet.

This is too new and unconventional to rock the
academic establishment. Few universities have even
started teaching mail order, and that's generally in
their community education offerings. Then, when you go
to mail order in the *Information Age*, there's no one
else teaching it. But you can get it today, in time to
get rich from it.

By the time the universities start teaching it,
it'll be dead. Like the dinosaurs. Like John Lennon in
literature class.

The *Mail and Grow Rich* System is the only way
known to man to get your hands on the actual "nuts and
bolts" of the process, ...

You get all the latest marketing discoveries - all
the newest tricks, psychological ploys, and stealth
devices *proven* to work to the tune of *billions of
dollars!*

It includes dozens of specific low cost high-
leverage strategies to make the *internet*, advertising,
direct mail, and *publicity* pay off better than Vegas
and Monte Carlo!

You get the same checklists I use to make
absolutely certain all my letters and promotions work
their guts out! Amp up <u>every</u> <u>single</u> <u>component</u> of your
marketing processes, experiencing quantum

breakthroughs to the magnitude of 300%, 500%, and even 5,000%!

The *Mail and Grow Rich* System is so hard-hitting, no-nonsense, and practical that some have called it a whole "University Program in 1 giant system."

But you can't learn this in the university. Not even in an advanced *M.B.A.* degree!

And there's another important contrast –

- **When you graduate from the university you still need The *Mail and Grow Rich* System.**

- **When you finish The *Mail and Grow Rich* System, you don't need the university.**

Completely New Material!

This is completely new information, not revealed anywhere else at any time at any price. You won't find the techniques we teach you in any book, video, or seminar... You won't find the insider's story like you find it here anywhere else. How could you? Even many people who were true giants in the 80's and the 90's don't "believe" in the internet. But the world of the 21st Century is the age of instant and cheap communications.

We get 35% of all our orders directly from our web site. Clients complete the online enrollment form and press "send" Others call and order, others print off the form and send it in. A whopping 60% of our total business concerns the web in some manner.

Yet the oldsters didn't even have it, and then, when it came around, most of them were already satisfied with the millions they'd made, and didn't go exploring this new medium. But the internet is here to stay. And there's nobody teaching it who's had such balanced success with it as I have.

Mail order has gone beyond the horse and buggy days, when it truly was "mail" order. Telephone sales didn't even exist back then, much less fax, the computer, the internet, overnight delivery services, and publishing-on-demand down at the neighborhood copy shop.

The modern mail order success makes use of *EVERYTHING* that will help him or her be successful. And the modern mail order entrepreneur has all these tools closely, easily, and *affordably* at home. It's truly amazing! Never before in history has it been so

easy for the little guy to get so easily and rapidly
rich!

In The *Mail and Grow Rich* System you get
everything you need to be successful in "mail order"
today –

> **A simple, step-by-step, fail-safe, screw-
> up proof, quick to implement,
> professional product development system
> and marketing campaign that anybody can
> use.**

**It's all laid out for you. <u>Nothing</u> <u>is</u> <u>left</u> <u>to</u>
<u>chance</u>!**

**Everything in this powerful course has been proven
in the marketplace. There is no textbook theory, no
wishful thinking, and no fluff or filler. It's all
hard-hitting, proven strategies and techniques that
have sold countless millions of dollars worth of goods
and services.**

You learn from me as I cover every itty-bitty
detail of direct mail, from ground zero to a complete
Million Dollar rollout! Your step-by-step plan for
success. Every "*i*" has been dotted, and every "*t*" has
been crossed. All the hard work has been done.

Best of all, it's a system that anyone of average
intelligence can do. I've made it all so simple that
it's like *connect-the-dots*... Sure, you'll have to do
a little work... nothing good ever comes without
effort, but the work you do won't be difficult...
Quite to the contrary... It's *fun*! It's a *challenge*
you'll love to take on!

Your whole life will transform overnight into a
passionate adventure, as you move confidently from
success to success! That's what we mean when we say
mail order can make you happy, healthy, and rich!

**You can get started without spending 1 single
penny**! Without pestering your friends. Start by
placing a free ad, perhaps on the internet. Pyramid
your profits from there. Unless you get blasted by one
of those F-14's, your success is guaranteed.

All you need to do is to learn how to write a
classified ad that gets attention. There are dozens of
secrets contained in a 22 word ad. You get them *ALL!*

And there are hundreds more secrets to the
construction of a kick-butt sales letter or display
ad... You get the whole boatload!

Not only that, in the unlikely event you do have a question, I am as close as your phone, your fax, or your email... Another vital weapon in your arsenal of success.

Start Today, No Matter What Your Present Situation

You learn exactly what to do if you would like to get into direct marketing today and earn $100,000, but don't have a product and don't have any money. It really is the *possible dream*. In fact, most of the giant direct marketing successes started just this way!

If you haven't read Ted Nicholas' "Message To Friends Who Want To Be Millionaires" closely, immediately after faxing, phoning, mailing, or e-mailing in your enrollment in The *Mail and Grow Rich* System, flip back to the bonus section and read it again, marker and pen in hand. You'll get a whole new, deeper, meaning from it the second time around! In fact, if you're like me, you'll refer to it every few months just to stay on course...

What This Program Is Not!

By the way, I guess it's because so many people have ended up with a garage full of vitamins, water purifiers, or soap that they ended up throwing away... or that they've already tried pestering their friends, sacrificing night after night when they should be *enjoying life* with their family... that I get asked so often... "Is this multi-level marketing?"

My direct answer is, "No, this has *nothing* to do with multilevel."

By the way, I have heard the stories of a few people getting rich in multilevel... There's Rich deVoss, of Amway, for instance. A few people at the top of those programs do get incredibly rich... But many of them lose it all 100 times faster than they made it. Remember Herbalife?

I move in opportunity circles, and I've not known too many people even paying their own way in multi-level... Much less *making money!* By contrast, there's a crowd of millionaire marketers. We want you to join us in this realistic opportunity.

Nor is this a fluke thing that only happened to me - without any real rhyme or reason... that could never happen again! The laws of human nature don't change anymore rapidly than do any other natural laws. Just as the "law" of gravity works for anyone and everyone who applies it, the "law" of direct response value-giving works equally as well.

If you know the secrets and apply them, *anyone can get rich in mail order today*!

So then...

"If This Is So Good, Why Are You Willing To Reveal It To Others?"

If there's one question which people both *want* to ask, and hold back from asking at the same time, it's this one... But, the answer is simple.

Call it the maverick in me... Like Hank Williams, Jr., I've always been a tad wild and nonconformist. *"Tell me I can't, and I'll tell you I will!"*

But the truth is, the way this business works, sharing with you can't hurt me. But it can help me a great deal.

The same thing with you. The fact that I'm sharing it with you, won't make any difference to the others I share it with, nor will the fact that I'm sharing these secrets of mail order with millions of people, through my books, articles, and media appearances, make any difference in your fortunes.

You see, mail order is a way of doing business, and then *optimizing* it is a way of leveraging yourself into assured success.

But there's enough wealth and enough variety in the world for *everyone* to be successful.

A butcher, a baker, a candlestick maker... First of all, when people ask why I would share this valuable information, they do so with a misunderstanding of exactly what's going on in direct response marketing, whether it's cyber-charged or not.

The things I'm teaching you can apply to *any product or service* and be successful. The odds that you and I will go into direct competition are *very slim*. Likewise, that you'll be in direct competition with anyone else who learns these secrets is equally remote. We can live with those chances.

We find an apt comparison in the world of sports. Though my game may be basketball (or business opportunities), I'm teaching execution skills (direct response marketing) that are going to make you better in your own sport.

Training people who apply the skills they develop to football, soccer, baseball, golf, tennis, racquetball, mountain climbing, running, etc., supplements, medical supplies, fine art, real estate, mortgages, exercise equipment, lingerie, dating services, foreign languages, computers services, investments, dentistry, chiropractic, and etc. won't ever affect me.

And even when I do train the occasional basketball player (business opportunity marketer) - it's a big world, and I'm up to the competition.

Why? Well, with the very secrets you learn in The *Mail and Grow Rich* System you learn how to *distinguish yourself* so that you never really have any competition. Guaranteed. Anybody who tries to imitate you is just that, an imitator. Someone who is savvy will develop their own strengths, interests, and opportunities, not yours. Not mine.

But, even that's not it... The *real* reason is *$ales*. Money. Profit. Gain. ...If you've been humanistically influenced, I apologize for offending you with these banal words, but for people who've got marketing in their blood, these aren't dirty words! They're making music!

♪♩D.S.♪ P♩♪C♩♩♪ ♪♩D.S.♪ s♩♩♪s

Historically I've found that I've either made purchases from or made sales to every one of my joint venture partners. I'm making a respectable profit on these sales, and I'm delivering *exceptional value* in every product. Or I don't offer it.

And every course I've bought (from someone I later joint ventured with) has paid me back in spades!

What we're talking about, Amigo, is living our motto, "Every friend is a friend for life."

I use the course to actively look for partners in further ventures. I'm hoping that you and I will do a string of deals together, for the next 10-20 even 50 years and more (your grandsons and mine). *Mutually profitable!*

Besides, as more and more people achieve financial freedom, that's *good!* They have more money to enjoy life and to improve themselves, spending that money with you!

Finally, and most important, it gives me genuine pleasure to see you succeed. It may sound funny to you (before the exercises in The Protégé Program), but I live to see you succeed.

It doesn't take anything from me to help you be successful. But it's the blood of my very purpose for living!

Your Mind-Blowing *Mail and Grow Rich* Curriculum

Your curriculum in The *Mail and Grow Rich* System consists of a structured system of 5 modules, 4 complementary advanced reports, plus a 6-audio cassette program.

The 5 high-powered modules you get are:

1. The "Business" End Of Your Million Dollar Mail Order Business

2. How To Get Your Own Million Dollar Product

3. Your Multi-Million Dollar Marketing Program

4. The Workhorse Of Your Multi-Million Dollar Mail Order Empire – *The Sales Letter*

5. How To Use The Internet To Make Your First Million Dollars

As you'll soon see, we're throwing in A *LOT* of other goodies, but the core of the course is in these 5 modules, loaded 8½" x 11" pages, conveniently spiral-bound so you can read and study them anywhere.

From Paycheck To Profit$

Module 1, "The "Business" End Of Your Million Dollar Mail Order Business," lays out the nuts-and-bolts of starting, running, and expanding your mail order business. This is stuff you need to know, stuff that, while admittedly not as "romantic" as the glitz of a successful marketing campaign, is indeed an essential component in your multi-million dollar success.

Even if you're a business dummy, you'll learn the effortless, stressless way to choose a company name and organization. You'll learn how to open your first checking account, and set the "attitude" you want your company to have.

Even though I'm not an attorney, tax advisor, or a C.P.A., you get sound business information and advice on how to comply with the various taxing bodies you'll encounter in your mail order career, like specifically the I.R.S. and the revenue department of your own state or province for remitting sales taxes you collect.

What you're getting are my professionally biased opinions as a successful businessman information direct marketer.

While especially designed for *newbies*, veterans alike will benefit in 41 pages of pure meat.

After all, it never hurts to remind ourselves that the word *business* comes from the root word *busy*. *Tend to your* "busyness" *and freely enjoy the riches that shower down on you.*

Value: $149.

How To Get A Million Dollar Product For Free

Module 2, "How To Get Your Own Million Dollar Product," simplifies the process of getting a product. Reveals everything in 106 pages.

Most people feel overwhelmed... But there's only 2 choices you'll ever need to make. It's an easy "either-or" decision.

You'll learn why selecting your product is the most important business decision you'll ever make – and how to avoid the nasty fate of the 95% of business owners who make this decision blindly.

You'll learn how to get started in a minute with resale and reprint rights to proven products, using proven marketing materials, and then, when you've got a few dollars coming in the door, how to get really rich by owning the exclusive rights to a product you create or acquire.

Then, as regular as the toll booth, <u>you</u> collect a portion of every sale that's ever made, anywhere in the world!

Completely Eliminate All Competition

Your heart will be pumping like crazy when you read this module and discover an ingenious but little known secret that absolutely 100% *ELIMINATES ALL COMPETITION!*

You'll see how easy it is! You can create a great *exclusive* product in a weekend, or buy one for less than $250... or get one absolutely free! And go on to make millions! You'll learn the secrets in Module 2, "How To Get Your Own Million Dollar Product." Value: $237.

Market-Centered Marketing Paves Your Road To Riches

Module 3, "Your Multi-Million Dollar Marketing Program" introduces you to the true secret of successful marketing - one that most beginning entrepreneurs, writers, and speakers are completely oblivious to. It should be child's play. It guarantees your success!

This revolutionary new concept - blazoned from page 1 to the conclusion of this powerful module - forms the base of all successful marketing.

P.S. Just so you'll know how important market-centered marketing is, if you ignore this principle, and do everything else perfectly right, still, you will fail. But if you hit the nail on the head with this principle, you can do everything else poorly, and still be a great success!

Marketing *is* *where* *you'll* *make* *your* *money.*

When you step forward to claim your millions, you need to select the kind of product that will indeed quickly, easily, and surely make you rich.

But what actually makes the money is promoting your product effectively through every *profitable* marketing channel at your disposal *to the right people*. That's *marketing!* That's *money! That's* the focus of The *Mail and Grow Rich* System.

This is your chance to learn the whole story of information marketing today. Your chance to learn from the masters. Your doorway to achieving the same levels of wealth and self-fulfillment they have! Inside this module you get concentrated, no-nonsense instruction from some of the most successful mail order marketers alive today. Men such as Ted Nicholas, Gary Halbert, Ted Ciuba, Bob Serling, Ted Thomas, Brian Keith Voiles, Michael Kimble, and a host of other heavy hitters.

Besides enjoying immediate success, you'll learn the secrets of lifetime "prosperity"!

You Don't Have To Work Hard To Make A Lot Of Money. All you have to do is learn how to set up your own direct response autopilot marketing system that will let you vacation in Florida or Lisbon and still have customer's money flooding into your bank account! Earn thousands while you vacation!

You'll learn how to use 800 numbers, voice-mail, and free-recorded messages so you have a virtual "office staff" on hand 24 hours a day! Knowing these deceptively simple savvy secrets are what will help you run your business on autopilot! You just check in occasionally by phone or email, no matter where in the world you are! PLUS, these telecommunications tools these days are so cheap and incredibly effective!!! 123 pages tells all!

Many people get hurt with mailing lists... Others thrive with them. You learn the simple secrets of success with mailing lists. There's loads of old, stale, and outright fraudulent mailing lists floating around out there. *Stay away from bargain lists!* Even many "reputable" list brokers will be happy to sell you the wrong list. *Nobody* will ever have your interests at heart the way you do.

You'll be fully informed in this vital area! Learn exactly who to go to rent lists. You see *actual* data cards, and learn how to *ask the right questions* so you won't be taken in by fastbuck artists. You will get rich quickly investing your marketing dollars in paying lists!

Indeed, today, the little person in his home office (even if that's the kitchen table), IS competing on a level playing field with the multinational giants! Learn how to hire out lead-taking services, mailing services, database services, so that you out-position, out-maneuver, out-smart the lugubrious corporate giants at every turn.

You Cannot Fail

Get the real inside scoop on "failure" in the direct marketing industry! Understanding and adopting this one distinction guarantees your success! Make sure you're alert when you read Module 3, "Your Multi-Million Dollar Marketing Program," because it can change your life.

Learn how to test small, and then *roll-out* a WINNER everytime! It's easy! Make *millions!*

Value is far greater than its retail of $297.

You Get 2 More Valuable Reports Worth $344 *FREE!*

Valuable Special Report, Yours Free With Module 3:

"High Impact Backend Marketing"

Value $197. In this valuable 110 page report you learn exactly how to set up joint venture deals that can earn you hundreds of thousands of dollars. I'll show you step-by-step negotiating strategies and give

you _actual_ _real-life_ _written_ _agreements_... Definitely
what's happening _on_ _the_ _street_ _today_.

Once you truly understand the benefits to both
sides of a joint venture arrangement, you'll suddenly
discover _hundreds of thousands_ of dollars in product
and dynamic marketing materials that can be _yours for_
free! Never get turned down.

Here's the attitude that'll make you a _FORTUNE!_

"Get rich together"

Cooperation, rather than _competition_, is the self-
serving way you can increase your own wealth in the
new business models of the Information Age.

"Backend" marketing is an essential pillar of
income in your marketing Parthenon.

This Is Included In Your FREE Special Report:
A Simple BIG MONEY Strategy

Folks, I've heard "Get paid while you sleep," and
it's good. I've heard, "Work _smart_, not _hard_," and
it's good. I've heard, "Let your capital work, not
you."

I believe in them all. But the one that pleases me
most is:

Get paid while others work!

You'll think you're in paradise – and you may be!
– when **you've got an army of motivated people working**
hard to make _you_ money!

Hang on for this profitable adventure, because
you're about to discover exactly how to set up your
own _network_ _of_ _distributors_ that will do all your work
for you and earn you thousands. How about having one
of your own distributors earning _you_ $99,629?! And
then keep on earning you more and more for years?

You saw the full story in chapter 6, "The
Principles of Wealth," and now you're going to learn
exactly how to put these powerful principles to work
in your _own_ business and life!

"_Get rich together._" There's a reason why this
system works so well! _You can build ongoing sources of_
tributary income through distributors only because
you're making it good for them, too.

In helping others profit, you profit.

True _win-win_

Truly a situation when teamwork and individual performance benefit *ALL* parties to the transaction.

You'll get the full, explicit, secret details – you'll even see the actual documents I use – so you can duplicate exactly what I've done. ...and have 10-12, or 25 distributors sending you money every day of the year!

Learn why this concept works so well, and exactly how to unleash its power into your own golden vaults.

Churning out thousands of dollars for you while you *enjoy* life!

EXTRA!

A Second Valuable Special Report, also FREE With Module 3, "Your Multi-Million Dollar Marketing Program" –

"Million Dollar Publicity Strategies That Don't Cost You A Dime ...and Make You *Millions!*"

Value $147. If you really want to maximize your marketing investments, how about spending 9¢ to send a fax and getting $75,000 worth of coverage? Or over $3 million dollars worth of sales from a *free* article?

I guess you know that publicity doesn't just "happen." But neither is it exceptionally difficult to stimulate. Getting publicity is a lot like riding a bicycle. Once you know how, it's easy. Before you know how, it's impossible.

Learn how to write publicity releases that get your product noticed! Fifty-six almost lethal pages reveal everything! Harness the power of publicity to scoop in the riches in your own career.

All About The Sales Letter, The Most Important Document In Your Business

Module 4, "The Workhorse Of Your Multi-Million Dollar Mail Order Empire – *The Sales Letter*" is the workhorse of The *Mail and Grow Rich* System. This giant 176 page study and permanent reference module dwarfs some of the others. Especially when you combine it with it's 2 supplementary manuals – *525 pages combined!* – Like Jupiter and Venus. (I guess there's a lot of hot air in a good sales letter...) As you'll learn, the sales letter is the most important document in your business!

But that's not all!

✔ You get 19 different and specific salesletter checklists to guarantee all your sales letters are chart-busters! A check list to guide you through every process of the sales letter from the elusive "feel" to the concrete *offer*!

✔ You learn how to decide whether or not you should have teaser copy on your envelope! And *double* your sales!

✔ Learn to incorporate the 6 functions of a headline in every headline you write. Your headlines will become money magnets when you get these right!

✔ You get 7 magic proven Million Dollar Sales Letter Formulas in the course, including Ted Ciuba's *Private* "No-Brainer Salesletter Formula."

> *The most financially lucrative skill you can possess is the ability to write effective sales copy.*
> – Ted Nicholas

✔ You discover one thing you can put in your sales offers that has never failed to increase response!

✔ You get the very latest 21st Century insider secrets and techniques that makes your mail stand out, and buyers buy!

✔ You never have to suffer the indignity of defeat. You learn which 1 type of book is guaranteed to sell... Nothing else – not even good literature – will make you money like this!

✔ When you understand what they are, you learn how to unleash powerful psychological principles that make your sales letters irresistible!

The Headline Alone Can Spell The Difference Between Failure and $uccess!

In fact, it's one of the greatest leverage points you'll ever encounter! If you truly know what you're doing, and how to do it, you can immediately write killer headlines to sell the dickens out of any product, winning *100%*, *900%*, and even *2,100%* more sales without spending 1 thin dime on additional advertising!

Valuable Special Report, *free* with module 4:

"How To Dream Up Hundreds Of Your Own Million Dollar Headlines"

Value $297! This special study concentrates solely on headlines – the most important element of a sales letter's success. You'll see indisputable publically printed *proof* that the Millionaire Masters themselves are "testing" headlines all the time. And that *you* should do likewise!

> *If you can come up with a good headline, you are almost sure to have a good ad.*
>
> *...But even the greatest writer can't save an ad with a poor headline.*
>
> – John Caples

If the headline is 90% of your ad, and if the headline can *easily* make a 300% difference in response, then this may be the most important component of the entire *Mail and Grow Rich* System! When you need ideas to write your own headlines, you'll find specific headline ideas and starters, along with over 100 of the **best-selling headlines of all time**.

P.S. No need to wait! If you want to bootscoot your boogie right now to **350** of the most powerful winning headlines of recent history, just point your browser to:

http://www.mailandgrowrich.com/free/350headl.htm

(You'll miss the in depth individualized discussion of the manual, but, hey, a good headline's a good headline!)

P.P.S. You gotta be country to understand the "bootscoot" boogie reference... But, don't you worry! Because Nashville's my home! I stage a number of international events right here in Music City. Want to visit the Grand Ole Opry? How about staying at the elegant Opryland Hotel? Ever dreamed of visiting Nashville's world famous Printers' Alley, 2nd Avenue at night, or Music Row? And there's more!

Like the world famous Temple of Athena, in famous Centennial Park. It's the Parthenon, located right here in the "Athens of the South." An exact (restored) replica of the ancient Parthenon on the Acropolis in Greece. Here you can *feel* the beauty and power of order and intention. The birthplace of many of the ideas that animate the *Parthenon Marketing* System. (P.S. After guitars, the Parthenon represents Nashville. There's 12 companies in the yellow pages that begin with *Parthenon*. Parthenon Marketing, Parthenon Futures, Parthenon Pictures, Parthenon Properties... etc.) Register in the *Mail and Grow Rich* System, and you'll get full details!

...As I was saying, you'll learn that it's perfectly legal to "steal" the ideas in these ALL-TIME SMASH HEADLINES for your own ads and letters! Not to mention it could be worth $1 million dollars to you.

You'll get 47 of the most powerful headline words and phrases that sell... and examples of how to use them!

You headlines will be bursting with power when you select from the 27 different kinds of headlines you can write! All market proven.

In 59 dynamic pages you learn to work and polish your own, but more importantly, you learn that - after your greatest excitement and efforts - you submit all your work to a conservative "test."

Then, when the market chooses which of your efforts it responds to best - in *Dollar$* and *¢ents* - all you have to do is open up another bank account to hold all the money pouring in!

A 2ⁿᵈ Valuable Special Report, Free...

"Killer Sales Letters For You To Shamelessly Copy, Mimic, and Bust Loose On Your Own Million Dollar Product$"

Value $199! You get a special beefy book that contains the full text of 35 different successful letters, postcards, display ads, and marketing plans from people such as Ted Nicholas, Brian Keith Voiles, Ted Ciuba, Gary Halbert, Ted Thomas, and Bob Serling, to name a few.

The models you get to copy - for *FREE* - in the 290 pages of this *kick-butt* manual, all told, have moved Billion$ worth of goods and services - 100% by direct response! **What can they do for you?**

You also get samples of sequential mailings, *sales* letter that accompany a refund... and more!

This is an invaluable resource, with killer examples - all market proven - that you can use as a fountain of endless inspiration!...

If you want to be successful, model SUCCESS!

All their most closely guarded secrets laid bare before your very eyes! Proven, tested, repeated, and improved! Model these letters, and unleash the power of the giants in YOUR promotions!

As They Say Around The Cow Lots of Texas,
"That Ain't Chicken-Feed"!

There's A Ton Of Things You'll Learn!

Here's just a *few* more things you'll learn inside the walls of Module 4, "The Workhorse Of Your Mail Order Empire – the Sales Letter":

✔ How a certain wording in your guarantee always lowers returns!

✔ Why to make all your letters look like a letter from home – and how to <u>get</u> <u>rich</u> <u>doing</u> <u>it</u>!

✔ 9 simple formulas for writing a killer P.S. that can <u>double</u> <u>your</u> <u>response</u>! This is working *smart* – not *hard*.

✔ Secrets that will make your order form strong enough to sell by itself! Even if your prospects never read the letter that came with it!

✔ The one <u>best</u> <u>way</u> to start your letter or ad.

✔ Which <u>one</u> <u>font</u> you should use in every letter you write and which one font you should use in every ad you write. (They're not the same!) Discover the no-brainer way you can tell what it is. *And watch your sales jump through the roof!*

✔ One simple, fun technique you can implement to double and triple response to your salesletters! Because you're dealing with human nature, this <u>never</u> <u>fails</u> to work!

✔ Why you don't need to worry about including postage-paid return envelopes in your mailings. If you've been doing it, this 1 tip alone will save you many times your small investment in the entire *Mail and Grow Rich* System!

✔ How to roll out a profitable direct mail project, *starting with 0¢ investment!*

✔ How to know *before you start* whether a project will be a mega success or a loser – and how to stop the losers dead in their tracks!

✔ How to get credit card payments processed no matter how bloody

> *After twenty-plus years in business, with 20-20 hindsight and clear present vision, it's obvious to me that, by far, THE most valuable skill is the ability to "sell via print".*
> – Dan Kennedy

your personal credit status is! Guaranteed!

✔ How to identify the best markets, poised to make you the most money.

✔ Where to find the best mailing lists to make you rich!

✔ The single most powerful word in the English language – or *any* language – and why you should sprinkle it liberally throughout your offers!

The Difference That Makes The Difference

You're going to discover the **big difference** between those who become outrageously successful in direct mail and those who fail miserably in life! It's a **single mental understanding** – yet it absolutely determines your level of success!

Harness the power of this one secret and your success is guaranteed!

You'll find this secret laced into every module, every tape, every video in the *Mail and Grow Rich* System! When you're ready to get rich, the world is ready to do it for you!

In this module you discover more of the killer leverage points in sales letters, and how to amp them up in every sales letter you write or approve so that you make 2-16 times more money!

Give me a lever and a place to stand, and I can move the Earth!
– Archimedes

And there's still more!

✔ 18 Power Techniques to build killer credibility that will flood your mailbox with high-dollar orders! Unleash these powerful ploys in your sales copy and prospects will line up in a boisterous crowd, drooling to do business with you!

✔ What the one perfect title is for any book or report you write. (You've probably never heard of this.)

✔ 22 magic "tricks" you can use to drive your customers to *buy NOW*. Believe me, if you *don't* play these tricks, there's no *magic!* You're leaving money on the table!

✔ The ideal length of a sales letter. (And it's not what you think!)

✔ The 25 biggest mistakes to avoid in salesletters. Laugh yourself all the way to the bank when you see your competitors committing them again and again and again!

✔ Which 12 important elements of a salesletter you can test... but not only that, the most effective sequence you should test these items in to maximize your return!

✔ Graphics can boost your response by 200-300% or they can trash it into the gutter... Grab hold of the 2 vital guidelines that guarantee your graphics will always boost response!

Value of this single module, more complete and thorough than most entire courses on copywriting, is $397.

The Internet's The Best Thing Happening!

With **Module 5, "How To Use The Internet To Make Your First Million Dollars"** you're pushing the envelope of technology... As such, you have to expect a little uncertainty... The terrain shifts as you travel over it...

But one thing that *isn't changing* is how much money you can earn rapidly and securely from the internet. It's nothing to earn $10,000, $30,000, or even $100,000 per month on the internet.

How many stories have you heard about it?

You'll learn all about how to do it – in the most up-to-the-minute module of the entire *Mail and Grow Rich* System! In fact, though the "current" version of the manual clocks in at a killer 80 pages, we're adding new sections and deleting outdated sections almost every month! Who can tell how many pages you'll receive? Your module will be *current!*

Addressed For Success

http://www.yoururl.com

What you *will* receive is the latest up to the minute details, strategies, resources, tips, and techniques that will help you maximize your marketing results with a minimum of time and money outlay!

Learn how to use email to build your business. How to design web pages that suck money out of visitors to your site.

Learn how giving away *free* services can build a repeat factor to your business. Learn how to use e-zines, affiliate programs, secure ordering, online credit card processing, and more. Models for everything.

You'll learn hów, you can operate your business entirely online, if that's what you want to do. (Though, of course, our Parthenon Marketing approach would suggest that you could make *more* money if you use other channels, too.)

The terrain of the internet may be shifting even as we speak, but one thing's certain... *The internet IS the new frontier of commerce.*

Fortunes are being made, almost <u>daily</u>!

Don't miss this! The internet is a key component in "Mail Order" in the *Information Age*. Value $377.

The *Mail and Grow Rich* System On Tape

Accompanying your written materials you get 6 jam-packed cassettes, the "*Mail and Grow Rich* System on Tape." Hey, if you're like me, it's flat *easier* to listen to cassettes... Anywhere, anytime. Running, dressing, or driving back home at 10:27pm on a Friday night. Really effective time management - effective learning.

But this is not just the course retold on cassette. The modules and the cassettes work together, separately and interdependently, to make you a master million dollar marketer.

I've pulled the best and the most immediate information, examples, and ideas from the manuals, organized them, and vitalized them with action information, ideas, and techniques not revealed in the modules. Here's what you get:

The *Mail and Grow Rich* System on Tape

Tape	Title
1.	Getting Started
2.	Marketing After A U.S.P.
3.	Strategic Direct Response
4.	Sales Letter Magic
5.	High Impact Backend
6.	Marketing On The Internet

Cassette 1: "Getting Started" – Want to know how to legally (that is "correctly") get started in business tomorrow? You'll quickly learn about licenses, proprietorships, partnerships, corporations, checking accounts, and more. You'll learn how to start with none of this. A bird's eye view of direct response marketing, you get the full picture, from product to profits, and all points in between.

Cassette 2: "Marketing After A U.S.P." – Once you know who you uniquely are and how you benefit your customers, you have the power to communicate it to your prospects. So you create your *Unique Selling Proposition*. This drives them to come seeking you out, and competition slides away to being a thing of the past! Join in with this session, and your business life will never be the same! It's essential you get this U.S.P. thing right to lift yourself beyond mediocrity into profound profitability. Once you get it, **you got it!**

Cassette 3: "Strategic Direct Response" – Above all, you'll learn that success doesn't come by accident. With marketing blindness we can't even see the mistakes we're making – though they're outrageous! This cassette will bring you marketing enlightenment. You *can* and *WILL BE* successful when you know what works and you do it. Find a good market. Find a product this market *wants*. Market to them effectively. The steps on the ladder of profits are test, test, test. When you *optimize*, your profits explode.

Cassette 4: "Sales Letter Magic" – If the sales letter is the most important document in your entire business, then it makes sense to become intimate friends with it, doesn't it? What elements make it work? What you absolutely must know about offers, bonuses, guarantees, and more! Headlines are at their best <u>spoken</u>. Once you hear a hundred well-turned headlines, an entirely new feel will animate your heart, and you'll find yourself endlessly spinning hundreds of headlines of your own.

Cassette 5: "High Impact Backend" – The success of any business is based on only 2 things. Everything else, including marketing that works, serves these 2 basic and essential secrets. Ever wonder why the business failure rate is so appallingly high? Most businesses have neither a clear, effective U.S.P. nor a firm *backend*. The successes do. You take care of the U.S.P. problem with cassette 2. In this cassette you get <u>7 different ways you can guarantee your future income</u> with backend vision today. You will prosper beyond belief when you see your backend as your <u>actual</u> <u>product</u>.

Cassette 6: "Marketing On The Internet" - Oh, yes, it's distinctly possible to operate your business <u>entirely</u> <u>online</u>. And make millions of dollars. More people are coming online everyday! You hear the stories of amazing success everywhere you turn. The future's bright! However, most major marketers would suggest the internet as a component of your information marketing business. Learn the inside secrets of driving *qualified* traffic to your site.

The retail value of the The *Mail and Grow Rich* System on Tape, your direct mail "university on wheels" is $247, but you get it <u>*free*</u> as part of your enrollment in The *Mail and Grow Rich System*.

When You Add It All Up

Put the pencil to this, and you can see that you're getting $2,544 worth of modules, manuals, and cassettes in The *Mail and Grow Rich* System! And even if it did cost that, instead of a fraction of that amount, it'd be worth it.

After all, what's a program worth that teaches you how to run your own $100,000 direct response information products business? What's a roadmap to the independent, wealthy, respected lifestyle worth? A fortune, right?

I think you'll agree that I went all out for you in The *Mail and Grow Rich* System. I've never heard of such value!

There's More

But, I'll tell you what - as complete as it is, I have to agree... there's one thing....

I thought and fretted and dreamed about this... Days running into weeks... On the pillow, in the shower, running in the park, at the office, in the air, on a boat... Even did a little day-dreaming in church.

I wanted something that would <u>literally</u> <u>force</u> any marketing student to become a marketing master. Believe me, this is an "educator's dream." I wanted my students to have the true ability, resources, tools, motivation, and mindset to make a *million dollar* income.

You see, one of the most critical aspects of benefitting from any new information, is the *ability to apply it*. Unfortunately, if you just read a book or just listen to a lecture - well, sometimes you leave with new ideas, but no actual techniques, strategies, and applications to your own real world.

In other words - *chévere* for the good time... but how is your business going to change when you're back there on Monday?

And that's where the advanced level of The *Mail and Grow Rich* System comes in...

Announcing!...

The MAIL AND GROW RICH
Protégé Program

Pushes you across that gap from "knowledge" into *action* –

The Protégé Program is 100% *PUTTING YOU THROUGH THE PACES, BUILDING YOUR OWN MARKETING PROGRAM... WRITING YOUR OWN KILLER MARKETING PIECES... SALES LETTERS, DISPLAY ADS, PRESS RELEASES CREATING EVERYTHING – FOLLOWING IN MY EXACT STEP-BY-STEPS WITH FILL-IN-THE-BLANKS EASE! – SO THAT YOUR OWN FORTUNE COMES ROLLING IN!*

Get The Skills You Need, To Quickly and Easily Roll Out One Millionaire Success After Another

I finally found what I was looking for - the magic bullet... Something that would take you by the nape of the neck and force you to *BE* a marketer. I felt I owed it to you. I found it.

Doing the Protégé workshop will put you in business. Making more money than you ever dreamed possible with your own products and services.

The Protégé Program is designed to make you a marketing master, a person with the skills and abilities to succeed independently. You won't need your old job very long!...

In it we work together - you and I - shoulder to shoulder, to design your own product and marketing

campaign. To write and polish your own direct mail
sales letter, publicity releases, and display and
classified ads.

The heart of The *Mail and Grow Rich* Protégé
Program is a set of contrasting manuals.

One is completely full, the other is almost empty.

One has my work in it – the entire *Mail and Grow
Rich* product and marketing campaign, from the ground
up... From the initial idea to the marketing strategy,
to the sales letter that sells the course. Lead
generation, backend, joint ventures, and distributors
– in a *real* case study. This is not a hypothetical
example.

It's titled "The *Mail and Grow Rich* Campaign
Workbook."

You learn exactly how I decide on my product, how
I outline it, and how I create it. You *see* me writing
ads, sales letters, and publicity pieces. Writing out
100 headlines, trying different offers... Until I
decide, and test. You see it all coming together...

And you participate. You see, **the other manual is
for you. This is the important manual. It has *your*
name on it. It has *your* work in it. This is for *your*
product! *WHATEVER* it is!**

**It's laid out so simply that you create your own
multi-million marketing campaign simply by following
along with me point by point, from idea to sequence
mailings, to thank you notes!... marketing strategies,
sales letters, guarantees... lead-generation, backend,
joint ventures, distributors... Everything from *idea*
to a *million dollars in the bank*, it's all there!**

In this course, you get *workbooks* – not
*read*books... Your work starts on the very cover of the
manual... Follow along with me... My workbook is
titled The *Mail and Grow Rich* Campaign Workbook. When
you receive *your* workbook, it'll look like this:

           "_____ Campaign Workbook"

You fill in the blanks... That's how easy it is!
But get used to it, because, modeling my documented
processes, you use your manual to develop your own
plans, processes, sales letters, joint venture
alliances, lead-generations, and sales processes for
your own success.......

This is truly a landmark work, one which you will look back on as a key point in your fortune-building career.

You move yourself from a belief or idea in your head to rolling down the highways paved with gold.

Nobody enjoys "study." Shucks, I know that nobody enjoys studying, and I don't know anybody who has any "spare" time in which to do it, either. I can't promise you won't have to work. That's why they call it a *work*book. But I'll tell you what! This isn't really "study." If you'll give yourself 6 evenings of intensely exciting involvement in your future in mail order – that's less than a week – you can literally transform your life!!!

In 6 days you can make the decisions and start the processes that will make you a millionaire.

Of course there's a trade off. If you don't think you'd enjoy prosperity, or if you don't think it's right to be rich, then perhaps this course isn't for you. If you'd rather have your life continue on the crummy way it's been going, then, resist the compelling urge to invest in this course and change your life.

I've never seen anything like this offered anywhere, at any time, at any price! Quite to the contrary, I've known a lot of people, including myself when I was first getting started, who would have paid a king's ransom for this insider information, *if it was possible!* You don't have that problem.

**What Would You Have To Pay To Work
Side-By-Side With
A World Class Marketer...
...*IF* You Could Find One
Willing To Let You???**

But yet, here you are! **Working on *YOUR* product or service, on *YOUR* marketing copy, side-by-side, following the same *ground-up* process of creation I use to guide a client or myself into a mega-successful product and marketing venture.**

We start at the base, with emotional thoughtfulness, developing a plan that will give you the money, freedom, love, and lifestyle you want. And these won't just be empty fruitless "wishes." We may be wearing feeling caps, but we'll be working with sharp pencils.

What I'm saying is that we'll get so basic that you'll write a U.S.P. even for yourself, as a person, so that you'll know what you want out of life... That's the foundation of your outrageous and *enjoyable* success!

Then we build up from there!

This is what makes you a true protégé.- you go beyond "reading" about it into *doing* it.

Together we choose a market, a product, and a marketing campaign, right down to the nitty gritty of the copy - headlines... themes... underlining, titling, italics, bold, big fonts... internal messages... the "call to action," the guarantee, and everything else that makes your copy pull like crazy!

It's like having Ted Ciuba design a bank busting promotion especially for you!... At peanuts of my regular fees. You get my full system - from the ground up: bright idea, research, product development, marketing plan, marketing pieces. This is priceless!

The *Mail and Grow Rich* Protégé Program is not just another "course," but a *practical guide to your success*. **It's all laid out for you. Follow along with me, step-by-step, from the ground up...**

If you're serious about success, you have to consider what I'm saying!

This is your chance! No exaggeration. Side-by-side, you craft your own sales and marketing pieces, thinking the same thoughts a world class marketer thinks for his own products. Get ready, because...

When you think like a world-class marketer, you produce *results* like a world class marketer.

When you've finished, you'll have your own fully *customized* marketing plan, ready to rain down millions on you. When you then launch your program and enjoy immediate success, write me... No kidding, we take the letters our affiliates send us, frame the best ones, and put them up on the wall! There's a space waiting for yours!

I'll Develop Your Product And Pay You Royalties

If, after you work your way through a rough draft with a product or idea of your own, you decide you don't want to develop it yourself, I'll even help you there. We're constantly on the look for products and campaigns to develop. If you choose this approach,

you'll have everything we need to really get in the
trenches with you.

We'll take your idea or patent, and spend *our*
time, resources, and money testing, developing, and
marketing it. All you have to do is sit back and cash
those fat quarterly royalty checks!

A Lucrative New Career

By the time you work through the Protégé manuals
you will have a new set of lifetime skills you can use
again and again to earn giant revenues anytime you
want.

Moving a direct marketing project stage by stage
to completion, you'll get a new view of the mail order
money business you're in!

You see *leverage* **built-in** to the project from the
beginning, and you see it progress. Then, you learn to
capture these outrageous leverage points in your own
business life.

When you've taken one program all the way from an
idea – nurtured, drafted, and crafted into a million
dollar fortune, you've learned something no school can
ever teach you! You've got the *marketer's mindset* that
can make you millions.

Indeed, as you work in the Protégé Program, it
works on you, and you become someone else. A master
marketer and killer copywriter. It's magical. You
don't just end up with a product, that is your own
marketing campaign and sales letters – your doorway to
millions – but you end up with powerful new marketing
and copywriting skills.

You can unleash these skills over and over again
during your life to roll out one success after another
for yourself and for your clients. To the tune of
million$ of dollars.

Course Includes Everything

I've made everything so simple that anyone of
average intelligence can follow it.

Includes *everything*, from conception, project USP,
sales letters, display ads, the test sequences, and
the publicity campaigns... With the course's work-
along forms you create your own program step-by-step
as you see my program come together before you.

You Can Do It!

There are no illustrations or examples that simply ask you to "learn".....

It assumes you have the basics down... It assumes you're excited, motivated... *and have two left thumbs when it comes to marketing and writing marketing pieces.*

Therefore, **this program is 100% PUTTING YOU THROUGH THE PACES, BUILDING YOUR OWN MARKETING PROGRAM... WRITING YOUR OWN KILLER MARKETING PIECES... SALES LETTERS, DISPLAY ADS, PRESS RELEASES CREATING EVERYTHING - FOLLOWING IN MY EXACT STEP-BY-STEPS WITH FILL-IN-THE-BLANKS EASE! - SO THAT YOUR OWN FORTUNE COMES ROLLING IN!**

BELIEVE ME! "Fill-in-the-blanks" was never so much fun - because this will be earning you MONEY!!!

"Please, Ted, Break It To Me Gently...

"What's All This Going To Cost Me?"

Let me tell you right up front that it's less - a *lot* less - than you might expect. You've already seen that the value of the materials you get with The *Mail and Grow Rich* System is a kool $2,544. The *Mail and Grow Rich* Protégé Program has a value of $7,505.

My marketing Mastermind suggested that I charge $1,997 for the *Mail and Grow Rich* System and $5,997 for the Protégé Program.

I could easily get that, perhaps even more. It's worth it. Remember, when I turn these materials and systems over to you - no hocus-pocus, no B.S., no baloney - **you have a $1,000,000 business**!

You can use your Mail and Grow Rich System to make Millions!

Up to that point, I'd been quiet... Then I said,

"Thanks, kind folks, for your input... But I've decided...

Not only will I *NOT* charge a lot of money for my programs, I want to make it even *better* for our purchasers..."

Suddenly the attitude changed. (That's the good thing about being the boss.) ☺

Where a few minutes earlier, they'd been huddling to figure out a "fair" price, they'd just got the ultimatum. I slashed the prices AND told them I expected a number of additional <u>valuable</u> irresistible bonuses thrown in for *FREE!*

The energy was high, everybody was feeding off of everyone else – out-doing one another to build up the value of your package, and drive down the investment you'd need to make. I think you'll be pleased.

But before I tell you about the truckload of valuable bonuses they chose for you, let's review what you're already getting...

With The *Mail and Grow Rich* System: Secrets To Getting Rich In Your Own Homebased "Mail Order" Business in the *Information Age* (That Apply To *Any* Business In The World!) you get over 1,000 pages! the entire tested, effective, and acclaimed 5 module *Mail and Grow Rich* course!

Total value of the <u>modules</u> alone equals $<u>1,457.00</u>

#	Title	Value
1.	"The "Business" End Of Your Million Dollar Business"	$149.00
2.	"How To Get Your Own Million Dollar Product"	$237.00
3.	"Your Multi-Million Dollar Marketing Program"	$297.00
4.	"The Workhorse Of Your Multi-Million Dollar Mail Order Empire – *The Sales Letter"*	$397.00
5.	"How To Use The Internet To Make Your First Million Dollars"	$377.00

Then, when you add on the 4 complementary special reports, combined retail value of $840.00, your value is up to $2,297.00!

With <u>module 4</u>, absolutely *FREE* – at <u>zero</u> <u>cost</u> you get:

• "High Impact Backend Marketing" $197.00

• "Million Dollar Publicity Strategies $147.00
   That Don't Cost You A Dime ...and Make
   You *Millions!"*

With <u>module</u> <u>4</u>, absolutely *FREE* – at <u>zero</u> <u>cost</u> you get:

With <u>module</u> <u>4</u>, absolutely *FREE* – at <u>zero</u> <u>cost</u> you get:

* "How To Dream Up Hundreds Of Your Own $297.00
  Million Dollar Headlines"

* "*Killer* Sales Letters For You To $199.00
  Shamelessly Copy, Mimic, and Bust
  Loose On Your Own Million Dollar
  Product$!"

Finally, you get The *Mail and Grow Rich* System on cassette! You get 6 audio cassettes in a beautiful organizer-binder. A real direct marketing University on Wheels... Learn this entire business from the convenience of your car, and just refer to the manuals for the forms, the ads, etc...

The value of this cassette program is $247.00, so, when you add it to the running total, your total value, *before any bonuses!* is up to $2,544!

The *Mail and Grow Rich* Protégé Program *Makes* You A *Deadly* Marketer!

The *Mail And Grow Rich* Protégé Program just like a roller coaster ride, changes your consciousness in seconds. You'd better strap in before opening the 2 key Protégé manuals. It doesn't just *share* marketing insights with you, but, pushing, guiding, inspiring, cajoling, thrilling you through a week's worth of exercises, <u>it</u> <u>makes</u> <u>you</u> <u>a</u> <u>deadly</u> <u>marketer</u>!

Here's what you get in The *Mail and Grow Rich* Protégé Program. To start with, you get everything in The *Mail and Grow Rich* System. All $2,544 worth.

Then you get the two manuals of the *Protégé Program*. First you get the thick spiral bound "The *Mail and Grow Rich* Campaign Workbook," which contains the insider, confidential, and *actual* documents used to design the *Mail and Grow Rich* products and marketing campaigns – all the strategies, ideas, drafts – in short, everything you need to mail and grow rich easily!

Value of this giant insider documentation is a conservative $1,297.

Second, you work along beside me in manual 2... The Manual which *YOU* title! It'll come with a blank

spot for you to fill in the title of your own
campaign! "_____ Campaign Workbook." Side-
by-side, you see what I did, and in your own workbook
you fill-in-the-blanks. This is where the magic
happens... Where the word takes flesh...

This manual is *not* spiral bound, but is a great
big 2½" looseleaf binder so that you can easily add
pages anytime, anywhere as your project develops!

This experience, and the resulting plan and copy
you end up with could easily cost you over $30,000 –
and you *still* wouldn't have the skills that you'll
acquire in this magic manual! It's very value-priced
at $1,977.

But don't worry, you won't have to pay that... Not
a *fraction* of that!

And at the end of the *Protégé Program* you'll have
your own marketing strategy finely tuned into a
<u>practical</u> <u>plan</u>, with every piece you need to apply it
– every sales letter and ad – ready to drop into place
immediately.

What *IS* a fair price for the *Protégé Program*?

The *Protégé Program* teaches you lifetime skills,
so that you become a millionaire with your own
products... But it also does *more!*

The *Protégé Program* gets inside your head and your
heart, so that you are transformed into a marketing
genius in your own right! You may even start a new
career, commanding the same high consulting fees I
command in your new business. I reveal everything to
you! You learn these valuable marketing skills, that
you get to keep *forever!*. You will have the ability to
exercise your skills again and again over the course
of you life, earning *million$!*

If you were a client, and I went to help you
create your own marketing campaign, <u>following the
exact plan and strategies</u> of the "Workbook," it would
cost you dearly. The diagnosis and strategizing
sessions alone, which may include site visits and a
week's work, could run you up to $17,000. The lead
generation campaign is another $15,000. Add on yet
another $12,000 - $17,000 for the sales letter. Of
course, I'd help you design and deploy a profitable
backend, including a sequence of letters to solicit
the original sale as well as benefitting from ongoing
sales to your current customer base, $12,500. That
totals up to $61,500.

Of course, if you contracted for all these services at the same time, I might offer some drastic discount, perhaps down to $22,297. But, don't forget, after a specified volume of sales, my royalties would kick in, and you'd pay me still more.

Needless to say, you probably can't afford me. Not if you're just beginning. Most can't.

But the ironic thing is that, even though I'm pricing your program a LOT, LOT, *LOT* cheaper, you'll be getting even more than I give a client! You see, my clients don't understand what I'm doing, why I'm doing it, or how it works.

They *can't* do it without me.

✔ But, <u>after doing it one time, you'll be able to duplicate the process over and over again</u>!

The possible return over a few years? More wealth than several people in several lifetimes could spend!

And you'll *never* owe me a single penny of your profits! (Unlike a consulting client, who could owe me a portion of his profits for years...)

The *Protégé Program* can make all your dreams come true. Literally, when you have a single hit, you can...

<u>Earn More Money In A Single Year Than Most People Earn In An *Entire Lifetime*</u>!

If you want these special prices, you'll have to act quickly. You see, my publisher is already nudging me to get my success stories organized for my next book. I need results in months, not years. Therefore, I can only promise to keep this low price open for a limited time. When I've got the stories I need, I'll have to raise the price.

But if you act quickly, I'll guarantee your spot at this great price!

Message To Friends

What could I possibly charge for The *Protégé Program* that would be a fair exchange for that?

Limited Time: Your Special Low Price

Fortunately, you don't have to pay based on the value of the information, the new skills, abilities, and level of income that you enjoy as a result of these courses.

That's, in fact, what makes <u>information marketing</u> so lucrative! Both the buyer and the

seller are satisfied at the transaction price! It's a
good deal for both!

In addition, I've got personal goals and ambitions
that suggest a lower price for the whole system.

You see, as a marketer/author, I'm already
planning my next project. For right now I want to get
a lot of programs out in the public and I want to get
their success stories. I'm looking for rags-to-riches
stories. The kind that this course creates. An
affordable price will do just that. A $5,000 price tag
would eliminate a lot of sincere people. I would only
be getting those who are already at least somewhat
successful in their own right now. Hardly the stuff of
rags to riches.

Your investment is fair, honest, and set at a
level that you can afford!

I've decided, for a limited time, that you can get
the entire *Mail and Grow Rich* System, with all the
valuable bonuses, and get it fully guaranteed, for
only **$497**!

And you can have the *Mail and Grow Rich* Protégé
Program, which includes all the materials in the *Mail
and Grow Rich* System **PLUS** all the extra goodies
outlined above, a total value of $7,505, for only
$997!

Yep, you heard it right... Only $497 for The *Mail
and Grow Rich* System and $997 for The *Mail and Grow
Rich* Protégé Program?

But there's more – a *LOT* more!...

If you are the type who can make a prompt decision,

**"Back The Truck Up, Baby, Because You're
About To Get A *Load* Of FREE Bonuses!"**

I think you'll agree I've already done well for
you! But if you'll order within the next 30 days, I'll
personally reward you with the *additional* following
valuable bonuses - all *FREE! ALL* at my expense!

Bonuses, Bonuses, Bonuses Like Crazy!

$1,687 Worth of *FREE* Bonuses
With Your Enrollment In...

The *Mail and Grow Rich System*

Listen, it's important to me that you feel – in every transaction' we ever do – you've genuinely gotten a *GREAT* deal! But, you surely agree, I've already given you 5-10 times your money's worth in this course...

I've already told you about the 4 special reports you get *FREE* with modules 3 and 4.

These valuable bonuses are in addition to that!!! I've decided, for a limited time, to throw in a truckload of valuable bonuses that you get to keep whether you send the course back or not!

FREE BONUS #1: Brian Voiles on the "AICPBSAWN" Formula

If "AICPBSAWN" sounds like the words of a magic spell, you've got it right! Former professional magician Brian Keith Voiles is today the world's top copywriter, and has engineered the success of some of the heaviest names in direct response marketing.

He reveals all of his important magical tricks with words in his famed home-study copywriting course, *Advertising Magic.* (Available from Parthenon Marketing, Inc.)

The basis for his success is his secret and proprietary "AICPBSAWN" formula. Brain plugs into this same formula to write killer copy for the world's heavy-hitters, and he reveals it to you!!!

It's like you're learning from the Merlin of advertising himself! He'll share specific techniques with you that can guarantee your success in today's skeptical society, as you

$2,600,000 From A Single Letter

Brian is absolutely the very best... that's why he writes my sales material. A 16-page sales letter Brian put together has brought in over $2,600,000 in the last 6 months for us. Those kind of results can happen only when someone knows how to write hot ads.
                                    – Mike Enlow

learn the touchstone elements of the *"art of human motivation."*

How much is a video tape that's only 22 minutes long worth? We offer it for $99, but it's worth *ten times* that!

The application of this formula earned Mike Enlow $2.6 million dollars in 6 months.

But <u>you</u> <u>get</u> <u>it</u> <u>free</u> with your enrollment, just for trying the *Mail and Grow Rich* System.

Extra! You also get a number of *killer* sales letters that Brian's written with your free special manual (accompanying module 4), *Killer Sales Letters For You To Shamelessly Mimic, Copy, and Bust Loose On Your Own Million Dollar Products!*

FREE BONUS #2: Million Dollar Mail Order Resources Rolodex

Normal selling point: $297. Value: *priceless*. It doesn't matter who you are, you can't do this business without this hard-to-find information.

Want to accept credit cards but don't want to go to the hassle of getting an account in your own name? You'll find the name, address, and phone number of <u>several</u> different companies – and the instructions to find up to 100 more with a single hour's research – who will take your customer's credit card info and process the billing *on their own account!* Starting *tomorrow!*

With the "Rolodex" you've got a working compendium of <u>people</u> <u>currently</u> <u>in</u> <u>the</u> <u>business</u> helping other mail order moguls like you get *rich*! Sure, you'll find the copyright office in here... but this is *NOT* just a compilation of old free information. Books, courses, fulfillment services, merchant services, personalized mailings, lettershops, printers, audio and video duplicators, specialized direct response software, premiums, ISBN... You'll find all this and more!

Every copy is *FRESH!* You see, this is the same working directory I use myself. When you order, we print up a new, fresh report – off of my computer – staple it, and send it to you. I don't know how to get you any more up-to-date tools and resources than that!

You can't do the direct marketing business without these contacts, and you get to keep this valuable bonus even if you send the course back!

FREE BONUS #3: Fax Marketing Critiques

Help When You Need It. Assistance is as close as your fax machine. Fax me your questions or your marketing ideas or pieces. What changes can you make, perhaps just a headline, for more sales? How about it, is your offer truly irresistible? I'll look at these things – and more – and give you my expert advice. I usually get $250 for each critique, so you're getting a $500 value which, for a limited time, I'll include *free* with this offer.

FREE BONUS #4: 1 Year Subscription To Marketing E-Zine
                                              Value $297

Simply by giving us your email address, we'll start your *free* subscription to the **"Mail Order" in the *Information Age*** e-zine. This valuable weekly resource keeps you informed and updated on product and marketing issues and opportunities in the direct response industry today. Online and *offline*.

P.S. If you'd like to start your subscription *today*, FREE, then surf right now up to http://www.mailandgrowrich.com and subscribe online.

FREE BONUS #5: 1 Year Subscription To Marketing Newsletter   Value $297

Valuable Bonus: You'll also stay tuned in with the industry through the special 1 year *BONUS* subscription to The *Mail and Grow Rich* Action Strategies Newsletter. In it I discuss different critical issues of technology marketing, as well as product and marketing ideas that apply to any direct response enterprise. Just one idea can sometimes earn you $20,000-$30,000 in a month's time. And in the course of a year you'll get *hundreds* of profit-laden ideas... Enough to earn an extra $1,000,000!

Worth its weight in gold!

FREE BONUS #6: Accept Credit Cards With Your Own Merchant Account   Value $197

To be a success in the direct response business, you've got to accept credit cards. You can capture impulse sales. Many people won't order if they have to go to the trouble of writing a check, filling it out, and sending it in. But if they can pick up the phone and call, you've captured it! But don't go where you do your banking. They'll have a mountain of reasons why they can't help, and why you'd better reconsider what you're contemplating.

I'll give you no-fault introductions to 2 of the highest rated, lowest fees, merchant-oriented credit card processors serving the domestic and international markets. 99.5% of all applicants are approved within 2 days!

The value of your bonuses is an incredible **$1,687**, yours *FREE* with your enrollment in The *Mail and Grow Rich System.*

EXTRA!

Limited Time $2,585 Worth of *FREE* Bonuses With Your Enrollment In The *Mail and Grow Rich* Protégé Program

I can't wait to share all the bonuses you get with the Protégé Program! You might think you're dreaming... Just gander at these killer bonuses!

FREE BONUS #1: Excel Direct Response Spreadsheets

The direct response business is a business of numbers... *Want more money? Mail more mail!*

These 9 spreadsheets are the very ones you use in The *Mail and Grow Rich* System. Makes planning, tracking results, and optimizing profits a snap. Just enter a few key figures, and the entire project is automatically calculated for you. Regular price is $397, and, worth it, because it can make or save you 10x that the very first time you use it!

FREE BONUS #2: 1½ Hour Video: Mark Victor Hansen Reveals "How To Use Your Mind To Make A Million Dollars"

Mark Victor Hansen, co-author of *Chicken Soup For The Soul* needs no introduction. Since he's also the co-author of *Chicken Soup For The Soul, A Second Helping; Chicken Soup For The Woman's Soul; ...For The Country Soul; ...For The Nickelodeon Soul;* and a host of others. THIS IS *CLASSIC* FOOTAGE. He's one of the world's best-loved motivators. You'll see Mark, enthusiastic and filled with big plans... *before* he achieved the stellar success he enjoys today. In 1994.

Which is what you'll *really* see – *Mark's success rolled out all by design.* When you watch and hear Mark, he'll share his plans for the "future." Of course, you today have that same vision today as accomplished past.

So, how so you use your mind to make a million dollars?... I've already said too much, and I don't want to give it away... But you'll sure see that spectacular success *IS* within your reach in the *Information Marketing* business! Mark, captured *before* it happened in his life, is the best testimonial you could ever have!

I think this is such an important presentation that I gladly paid $5,000 for the rights to give you this tape. It sells individually for $197.

P.S. One quote: "You write a good book – that's 10%; *marketing* is 90%!"

FREE BONUS #3: In Person Consultations with marketing genius Ted Ciuba

In Person "No Holds Barred" Personal Assistance From Me. You get two (2) 30-minute Master Mind phone consultations directly with me. These focused, dynamic sessions can mean the difference between so-so results or a million dollars! *Be sure and use these most valuable sessions!* Before our conversation begins (by appointment, so there's no interruptions), you send in copies of your marketing materials and strategies, and we go to town!

I'll get hot and specific, telling you exactly what you can do to improve your product, your copy, your marketing strategies, your lead-generation, your backend, or whatever needs it.

Normal charge for 2 dynamic critiques is $1,500, but they could pay that back on your first day of a mail campaign...

P.S. You Must Act Today! I am committed to your success. Because of that, though time is my most valuable asset, I'll share it freely to help you be successful. Additionally, when you enroll you'll also receive my *personal* email address; I'll help you anytime you write. But I must warn you... So far, I've been able to personally respond to all requests for critiques and consulting.

But I can't do this forever. I may have to quit in a few months. At any rate, I don't intend on selling over 100 copies of the Protégé Program, just to keep from overloading myself (and cheating the people who pay good money to enroll!).

Be sure to get your own copy of The *Mail and Grow Rich* Protégé Program while you still get this valuable free bonus!

FREE BONUS #4: Internet Marketing Bulletin Board

You'll get priority membership privileges to our marketers bulletin board, a $197 value. Share ideas, thoughts, get feedback on what's working, or what won't. Make marketing friends, get critiques on your promotions... Invaluable resource, with others who are doing the business! – yours *free*.

**FREE BONUS #5: Outrageous <u>Additional</u> Bonus - *FREE!*:
Copywriter's Secret Session**

Come with us, and as easy as listening to a
cassette tape, learn how to incorporate the secrets of
a letter that's earned over...

Over $1.2 Million Dollars per WORD!!!

Yes, that's <u>PER</u> w-o-r-d!!!

P.S. You may have seen this letter... As incredible as
it seems, after 20 years! I actually received it in
the mail <u>today</u>! (After my presentation...) *Unchanged!*
If there was <u>ever</u> a killer sales letter, **this is it!!!**

With the cassette and the handouts you get, that
include my notes and the full text of "The 2 Richest
Salesletters In The World," you participate in this
secret session I put together for a presentation to a
high level Master Mind meeting, one in which a handful
of international attendees each paid $10,000 (plus
posh expenses) to attend.

Both of these letters have grossed over a *BILLION
DOLLARS* each!

Unleash their powerful secrets in *your NEXT*
promotion!

**You can't buy this report <u>anywhere</u>, not for any
amount of money!** ...and it's worth *BILLIONS!* Value? <u>I
don't sell it</u>, but *IF* I did, this one cassette and the
handout of a few stapled pages would go for $197, and
be *worth it!* But, dear friend and profitable partner,
as an educational benefit to people who prove
themselves ambitious, I'm giving it to you - *FREE!*
Just for checking out The *Mail and Grow Rich* Protégé
Program.

Whew! I've never heard of piling on bonuses like
that! Have you?!! The value of the Protégé BONUSES
ALONE exceeds $2,585!

When you add on the value of the two Protégé
manuals and the magical marketing alchemy they
perform, along with all the modules, manuals,
cassettes, and videos you get with The *Mail and Grow
Rich* System, you've got a Protégé Program <u>value of
$10,090</u>.

You'd better act quickly, before I come to my
senses and withdraw this special offer!

There Are No Limits On Your Guarantee

I really can't guarantee your income. That depends on too many variables I don't have any control over. For instance, if you never run an ad, how can you have success? But I *know* the methods and techniques you'll learn about *can* make you an easy $100,000 – just warming up! A multi-million dollar income is well within your abilities – if you act on the materials in The *Mail and Grow Rich* System and The *Mail and Grow Rich* Protégé Program.

So if I can't guarantee your income, what can I guarantee? My guarantee is as simple as it is rock-solid. I'll guarantee my course materials absolutely – without condition – for any reason.

I'll give you a full 30 days to look them over in the convenience and privacy of your home and make your own decision.

I'll send you the modules. I'll send you the tapes. I'll send you the special reports, the manuals, the videos, and ALL the bonuses (yours to keep whether you send the course back or not!). I'll reveal the secrets and hidden resources that have made others millionaires, and can do the same for you.

Then, when you have read, listened to, and watched everything in the entire program and decided for yourself that my materials, information, methods, and ideas are right for you... and that you are right for them, then we'll consider our deal final.. You and you alone decide whether The *Mail and Grow Rich* System or The *Mail and Grow Rich* Protégé Program has value for you.

How could I be more fair?

With my liberal 30 days no-questions-asked return policy, if *you* don't agree, send the course back to me in original condition for a prompt cheerful refund. No questions asked. We'll still be friends.

That's how serious I am. *You* be the judge.

How can you loose? The most you could be out-of-pocket on this offer is the shipping and handling, and frankly, if you don't think that small "risk" is worth what you stand to find in this system, then you're not the type who could be successful in this business anyway. I'll give the spot I reserved for you to someone else.

But I Do Have 1 Condition

The philosophies, principles, strategies, and techniques you learn in the *Mail and Grow Rich* programs are absolutely awesome. You learn to strategically unleash a whole network of powerful psychological principles of human persuasion. The power it gives you over other human beings is staggering!

That's my point... If you don't think you can be entirely honest and work for the well-being of humanity, then I absolutely refuse to sell to you.

Do not order.

Sure, it costs a lot... but if you think this course is expensive, compare its cost to its *benefits*

Of course I realize that $497 might seem like a big investment to you right now. If that's the case, think of the <u>value</u> of what you receive! There's literally *1,000's* of secrets you'll learn in the modules, cassettes, videos, workbooks and other bonuses you receive with your enrollment. Any *1* of these secrets could mean $100,000's of dollars of income to you!

Combined, it's awesome to think of their potential power! They can blast you - as quickly and as cleanly as making a quantum leap - into a situation that will make you and your family prosperous for the duration of the 21st Century!

Sure, this secret *but effective* knowledge will cost you a few hundred dollars... But compare this cost to the cost of education in general.

No, I'm not putting education down, but I do see the general purpose of institutionalized education is to "norm" you. Hardly the stuff of getting ahead!

They train people to be homogenized sheep, and then, with the fear of execution if you fail, they fit you (oh so happily, right?) into a little job somewhere, so that you never see how the big picture works.

You've likely already discovered that the dream of keeping up with the Jones is an illusion, and that mediocrity is no fun. Most people attracted to the *Mail and Grow Rich* philosophy have already reached the point of dissatisfaction saturation.

The Government Doesn't Want You To Have This Secret Information

The thinkers and do-gooders of government and social planning have seen what I'm doing and they've tried to settle me down. By some clever arguments, they're taking my own purpose of striving to help you become happy, healthy, rich, and independent, and telling me that it won't work.

They say I'm somehow "special."

> *Give me a stock clerk with a goal, and I will give you a man who will make history.*
>
> *Give me a man without a goal, and I will give you a stock clerk.*
> - J.C.Penny

"But Ted," they say, "not everyone can see as clearly as you do. Ordinary people won't be able to achieve the same levels of success you have, and then, instead of helping them, you'll actually be hurting them!...

...by building up their hopes and dreams and then disappointing them..."

I suggest to these bureaucrats that they go read Napoleon Hill's *Think and Grow Rich*. They'll encounter the basis of the book early in the *first* chapter:

"All who have accumulated great fortunes, first did a certain amount of dreaming, hoping, wishing, desiring, and planning *before* they acquired money."

I don't think they understand it.

I'll tell you what's "special" about me - *nothing!* But like every successful person in every walk of life, I've also had my reversals. You will too. The measure of a man is not that he falls short of a goal, but that gets up again and again until he reaches it.

Which touches on the real problem... Can you imagine a nation of **successful self-determining individuals**? The prospect is frightening!

Creativity, initiative, boldness, enjoyment - when's the last time you heard these subjects talked about at school? These traits and qualities are

> *It took me years to become successful; it happened in a few weeks.*
> – Ted Ciuba

NOT taught at school. Don't bother waiting... It won't happen, either.

If you want to be a sheep manager, following sheep rules, well, then more university "education" is perfect for you. A bank middle manager is the flower of the educational system.

A good education may cost you $100,000. I'm sure you agree that's a conservative figure. Then you'll get a job wearing a white shirt instead of a blue shirt, and an additional $6,000 per year. Sometimes.

You're trading earnings of less than $500 a month for 4 years of your life! And, though you may "statistically" be in a higher income bracket, aren't you still caught up in the same rat race? When, starting in a few days, for less than $500 - a mere 1/200th of $100,000 - you can enter the mail order business under the tutelage of one of today's most knowledgeable and successful mail order tycoons! Which do you think is a better deal?

Limited Availability of Protégé Program

I'm a very busy man. Running my own business, giving talks and workshops, community work, marketing consulting, writing another book...

And I've just taken on personal coaching for Protégés. The bad news is that I can't make this an unlimited offer - not at this price. I won't accept any more protégés than I can properly handle.

What does this mean to you? It means that these positions will fill up fast, so if you want in, you'd better act immediately.

If you drag your feet, and lose out on this opportunity, I'll add you to the waiting list. *Good luck!*

Plus, you're getting a special price with this offer, because it costs me less to handle your Protégé enrollment when you combine your enrollment with the *Mail and Grow Rich* System. Your net outlay for the million dollar materials in the *Protégé Program* is only $500. But if you order the *Mail and Grow Rich* System now, and wait on the Protégé Program, you'll have to pay $797 to get the Protégé alone. You save $297 by being decisive and acting *now*.

If you want to make sure you hammer down the opportunity to substantially increase your profits - right now and for all the years into the future - you'd better act <u>today</u>.

To order immediately call **right away** **toll-free 1-877-4 RICHES**. Business hours you can call +615-662-3169.

What You'll Have To Give Up If You Don't Enroll

If you still think you can't afford this course, or if you feel like you can wait, then you're probably not the kind of person who would be successful in this business anyway. So go buy a new portable stereo with the money instead. Throw in a few CD's. A stereo isn't likely to improve your financial future any, but then neither would this course.

You see, *Mail and Grow Rich* is designed to earn you a minimum of $100,000 per year. And if you want it, **millions**.

Stop and think about it... just how much is the lifetime ability to earn $100,000+ every year for the rest of your life worth? If you're 35 years old now, you can reasonably be expected to work another 30 years, especially since directing someone to send out a few letters and a few products each day is very light work indeed! That's a cool... $3 Million Dollars!

And this is what should concern you most! Not how much the course costs, which is only $1.36 per day, but how much you'll give up if you don't enroll! Cars, vacations, schools, true security, dining, travel, an expensive home, freedom, confidence, prestige!

Worst of all – you'll have to live with the knowledge that you never gave yourself a chance! *Can you afford to trade the present joys and the future well-being of yourself and your family for a bottle of beer a day? Can you risk that?*

Now I'm certainly not trying to push any religion – I have mine and I respect your choices – but if you decide to trade your future prosperity away because a few hundred dollars seems like it's too much money, you're playing out the Hebrew story of Essau choosing a pot of porridge over a millionaire's birthright.

That's how strongly I feel about this program and about you. That's why I've reduced the price so low and made it so easy for you to acquire it!

And I've even 100% guaranteed it so that, if you're not sure, you can still check it out in the privacy of your own home without any risk.

Isn't that what you <u>really</u> <u>want</u>?... The confidence
of knowing your future years are taken care of... <u>More</u>
freedom?... <u>More</u> passion?... <u>More</u> time with those you
love?... <u>More</u> travel?... <u>More</u> cash?

You and I both know that if you've read this far,
you have a <u>driving</u> <u>interest</u> in winning your own riches
in "Mail Order" in the *Information Age*. The time to
act is now.

This is a strictly limited offer. It's your
future, your life, your prosperity, and, right now,
it's your magic moment!

Mail and Grow Rich!

Ted Ciuba
Marketer, Marketing Consultant

P.S. In module 4 of The *Mail and Grow Rich* System
you're going to get the best sales letter formula in
existence. And guess what? I've just received a
limited number of printings of this killer formula
specially printed on the highest quality paper!
Designed to last for years! Stocks are limited, but if
you order within the next 10 days I'll guarantee you
can have your own *autographed*, suitable-for-framing
copy of "Ted Ciuba's Private 'Best-of-the-Best' No-
Brainer Has Everything Salesletter Formula."

Hanging on your wall it'll be a great motivator,
as well as a precision profit-producing tool you'll
never want to be without! Don't miss out on this *FREE*
valuable bonus! Register NOW!

**P.P.S. You Won't Believe This, But, Here, <u>IN PUBLIC
PRINT</u> (WHERE I *CAN'T* DENY IT) ... I've decided...**

I'm Giving You
$997 CA$H!

That's right!

This is my brainchild! It made my advisors
shudder! "Ted," they exclaimed, "you're going to
actually *GIVE* your Protégés almost $1,000 in CA$H?!!"

I'll tell you, if you want *this* bonus, then you'd better act *QUICK!*

Maybe I'm wrong in doing it, after all, it's going to be hard for me to make any money paying you back for your course 2 days after you paid for it yourself. But, if you order quickly, you're guaranteed this bonus.

(On the other hand, dally, and I can almost certainly guarantee you'll be too late. ...Don't hate yourself for missing out on this one!)

I'll explain everything in the special *Fast Start Marketing Plan* you also get with this bonus, but here's the quick scoop on how it works...

You've invested this much to get the Protégé Program. When you get your course, I'll include, *free*, 2 extra copies of *Mail and Grow Rich*, this very book. Sell each of these to someone who's interested – either a friend or someone you find by posting an ad (it can be free) almost anywhere.

When you give it to them, explain that, "If you're interested in any *Mail and Grow Rich* Advanced Training, get back with me! You see, I've got a 'resale license' for the courses, exactly like you get for the book, *Mail and Grow Rich*, and I make money when you order through me."

Nearly 100% of the people you make this offer to will be respectful enough to come directly back to you.

You already know how genuinely valuable the product is, how outrageous the bonuses are, and how killer the copy is. Closing is a snap. They'll just fill in the order form and give it to you with their payment.

> *Pursuit is what makes the difference. Reaching for what you want alters the odds immediately, and drastically of getting it.*
>
> – Price Pritchett

However, 50% of the money is yours! Just tell me where to ship the course.

Imagine that! You have *nothing* on the line! 2 courses and you instantly and absolutely *zero out* on your own valuable investment in the *Mail and Grow Rich* Protégé Program!!!

And, if you don't have credit card ability yet, don't fret a moment! We'll process the card, and send you your half.

NOTE: With this bonus I also promise to include *full details* on how you can get a permanent license to resell the *Mail and Grow Rich* courses – *and a whole Parthenon backend of highly prized and highly profitable courses* – backed up with <u>proven *KILLER* copy</u>. You can make a fortune with resale and duplication rights, and I'll give you the full rundown. A guaranteed bonanza!

I've pulled out all the stops! I've done everything I can, <u>including paying for your course</u>, to make sure that YOU are super successful in the shortest period of time! Now it's your turn.

P.P.S.S. I couldn't leave without being completely truthful with you. Most of the examples I gave in this book, including earning $100,000 per year, have been dramatically watered down. I wanted to be believable. When I talk about receiving $3,000 per day or $3,288.90 in less than 1 hour... *Nothing to it in this business!* I just got a call from a recent affiliate in Austin, Texas. Talking about receiving his mail, are you ready for this?! He had a few checks... In fact, he had...

$5,549 In His Mailbox...
In A <u>Single</u> Day!

– And that didn't count his <u>fax</u>, his <u>email</u>, or the orders that had come into the fulfillment center by <u>phone</u>!!! –

You have the same access to mail service, a fax, the internet, and the phone that he does!
All without ever leaving the house!
It's Your World –

"Mail Order" in the *Information Age*

Put the pencil to it... At this rate, even if he only worked one day a week, and didn't check his fax, his email, or his phone orders, and (since he has the ultimate life of leisure *and* money) he vacationed for <u>3 full months</u> of the year, he'd still be clocking in at <u>$221,960 per year</u>!

Double check me on this... What if he worked 4 days a week, and, since the money comes in whether he works or not, the 3 months of vacation don't really make any difference?

That's the easy way to hit the million dollar mark! $1,154,192. These are *ordinary people* who have acted on this *extraordinary opportunity* to get rich quickly, quietly, soundly, and permanently. Ordinary folks. Extraordinary income.

Why can't this be you?

It can! Your financial fate, everything you have to give your family and yourself, <u>everything</u> <u>depends</u> <u>on</u> <u>your</u> <u>decision</u> <u>right</u> <u>now</u>. This *can* be you – if you *choose correctly* <u>right</u> <u>now</u>!

> *In any moment a decision you make can change the course of your life forever...*
>
> *The very next person you stand behind in line or sit next to on an airplane,*
>
> *the very next phone call you make or receive,*
>
> *the very next movie you see*
>
> *or book you read*
>
> or page you turn
>
> *could be the one single thing*
>
> *that causes the floodgates to open,*
>
> *and all of the things that you've been waiting for to fall into place.*
>
> – Tony Robbins

Mail and Grow Rich Instant Application Form

Yes, I Want The Good Life I Can Have With "Mail Order" in the *Information Age*!

✔ Yes, Ted, I want to get rich quickly, easily, safely, and insanely using today's simple technology tools like the phone, a fax, my computer, and the neighborhood copy machine, working part-time from my home!

✔ Yes! There's going to be a new balance in my bank, a new spring in my step... a new gleam in my eye... and suddenly *jealous* neighbors!

✔ Yes!! Send me everything just the way you outlined it in *Mail and Grow Rich!* including my unconditional 30-day guarantee!

____The *Mail and Grow Rich* System. $497
- I get all 5 modules, the 4 advanced manuals, and the *Mail and Grow Rich* System on 6 cassettes. Value of $2,544.
- I also want all the bonuses you talk about, mine to keep even if I send the course back. All $1,687 worth of bonuses! Combined total value of $4,231.

_____The *Mail and Grow Rich* Protégé Program $997
- For starters, I get <u>everything</u> in the *Mail and Grow Rich System, PLUS* 2 transformative manuals, The *Mail and Grow Rich* Campaign Workbook, and my own manual, The _____ Campaign Workbook, conservatively worth $3,274.
- Then you're going to stack on all $2,585 worth of *Protégé* bonuses, which I get to keep even if I send your course back.
- PLUS, I get a Resale license to the *Mail and Grow Rich System* at 50%. Good for a full year till I earn back *every single penny I invest!* That's a *free* $1,297 <u>cash</u>! Combined total value of $11,387.

Tax for Tennessee residents (*System*: $41, *Protégé*: $82.25) . . . . _____
Shipping for GIANT package, add $27 priority, $60 overnight, $75 International_____
GRAND TOTAL . . . . $_____

It's Easy to Enroll – Call, mail, fax, or email this form or this information to us!   213

Name_____

Address_____

City_____ State/Province_____

Postal Code_____ Country_____

Phone/fax_____ Email_____

___Cash, check, money order   ___ Please charge Visa, MasterCard, AMEX, or Novus/Discover

You can spread your investment over 2 cards. Just tell us how much to process on each.

Card #_____ Exp date_____ Amount_____
Signature_____ Date_____

Card #_____ Exp date_____ Amount_____
Signature_____ Date_____

Parthenon Marketing, Inc.
2400 Crestmoor Rd #36
Nashville TN 37215   USA

Order Toll Free: 1-877- 4 *RICHES*
+615-662-3169 / fax: +615-662-3108
http://www.mailandgrowrich.com
mr@mailandgrowrich.com

For superfast processing rush this form or this info to:

Parthenon Marketing, Inc.
2400 Crestmoor Rd #36
Nashville TN 37215
USA

+615-662-3169 / fax: +615-662-3108
http://www.mailandgrowrich.com
mr@mailandgrowrich.com

Mail and Grow Rich Instant Application Form

Yes, I Want The Good Life I Can Have With "Mail Order" in the *Information Age*!

✔ Yes, Ted, I want to get rich quickly, easily, safely, and insanely using today's simple technology tools like the phone, a fax, my computer, and the neighborhood copy machine, working part-time from my home!

✔ Yes! There's going to be a new balance in my bank, a new spring in my step... a new gleam in my eye... and suddenly *jealous* neighbors!

✔ Yes!! Send me everything just the way you outlined it in *Mail and Grow Rich!* including my unconditional 30-day guarantee!

____**The *Mail and Grow Rich* System.** $497

- I get all 5 modules, the 4 advanced manuals, and the *Mail and Grow Rich* System on 6 cassettes. Value of $2,544.
- I also want all the bonuses you talk about, mine to keep even if I send the course back. All $1,687 worth of bonuses! Combined total value of $4,231.

____**The *Mail and Grow Rich* Protégé Program** $997

- For starters, I get everything in the *Mail and Grow Rich System, PLUS* 2 transformative manuals, The *Mail and Grow Rich* Campaign Workbook, and my own manual, The _____ Campaign Workbook, conservatively worth $3,274.
- Then you're going to stack on all $2,585 worth of *Protégé* bonuses, which I get to keep even if I send your course back.
- PLUS, I get a Resale license to the *Mail and Grow Rich System* at 50%. Good for a full year till I earn back *every single penny I invest!* That's a *free* $1,297 cash! Combined total value of $11,387.

Tax for Tennessee residents (*System*: $41, *Protégé*: $82.25) .... _____
Shipping for GIANT package, add $27 priority, $60 overnight, $75 International _____
GRAND TOTAL .... $_____

It's Easy to Enroll – Call, mail, fax, or email this form or this information to us! 213

Name_____

Address_____

City_____ State/Province_____

Postal Code_____ Country_____

Phone/fax_____ Email_____

___Cash, check, money order ___ Please charge Visa, MasterCard, AMEX, or Novus/Discover

You can spread your investment over 2 cards. Just tell us how much to process on each.

Card #_____ Exp date_____ Amount_____

Signature_____ Date_____

Card #_____ Exp date_____ Amount_____

Signature_____ Date_____

Parthenon Marketing, Inc.
2400 Crestmoor Rd #36
Nashville TN 37215 USA

Order Toll Free: 1-877- 4 *RICHES*
+615-662-3169 / fax: +615-662-3108
http://www.mailandgrowrich.com
mr@mailandgrowrich.com

For superfast processing rush this form or this info to:

Parthenon Marketing, Inc.
2400 Crestmoor Rd #36
Nashville TN 37215
USA

+615-662-3169 / fax: +615-662-3108
http://www.mailandgrowrich.com
mr@mailandgrowrich.com